DAY HIKES IN
VENTURA
COUNTY
CALIFORNIA

43 OF THE BEST

by Robert Stone

Day Hike Books, Inc.
RED LODGE, MONTANA

Published by Day Hike Books, Incorporated
114 South Hauser Avenue
P.O. Box 865
Red Lodge, Montana 59068

Distributed by The Globe Pequot Press
6 Business Park Road
P.O. Box 833
Old Saybrook, CT 06475
www.globe-pequot.com
1-800-243-0495

Photographs by Robert Stone
Design by Paula Doherty

Cover photo: Santa Paula Canyon, Hike 28.
Back cover photo: Paradise Falls, Hike 12.

TABLE OF CONTENTS

— THE HIKES —

SANTA MONICA MOUNTAINS
Circle X Ranch and Point Mugu State Park

THOUSAND OAKS
Los Robles Trail System and Wildwood Park

OAK PARK and AGOURA HILLS

MOORPARK, SIMI VALLEY and FILLMORE

CAMARILLO and VENTURA

OJAI and SANTA PAULA

About the Hikes

Ventura County, California, has a unique and diverse terrain with many hiking trails to accommodate every level of hiking expertise. This guide will take you to the best day hikes in the area, getting you to the trailhead and onto the trail with clear, concise directions.

There is an extensive network of hiking trails within the county's many parks, wilderness areas, and mountains. The hikes in this guide span from the Pacific Coast to the Los Padres National Forest, taking you to waterfalls, swimming holes, canyons, rivers, mountain peaks, extraordinary rock formations, caves, rolling meadows, and panoramic views. These beautiful areas can often be enjoyed for the whole day. To help you decide which hikes are most appealing to you, a brief summary of the highlights is included with each hike.

Many of these hikes are found within a short drive of the cities. An overall map of the county and the hikes can be found on pages 6—7. Each of the hikes is also accompanied with its own map and detailed driving and hiking directions. The U.S.G.S. maps and other supplementary maps listed with the hikes are not necessary but may be useful for some areas. Many of the U.S.G.S. maps have not been updated recently, and the trails may not be shown. However, these maps are interesting because they show the topography of the region.

Be sure to wear comfortable hiking shoes, and be prepared for inclement weather. A rain poncho, sunscreen, insect repellent, and drinking water are recommended.

From one end of Ventura County to the other, there is a range of sights and hikes. Whichever area you choose to visit, this county is rich in beauty and diversity, waiting for you to discover it out on the trails.

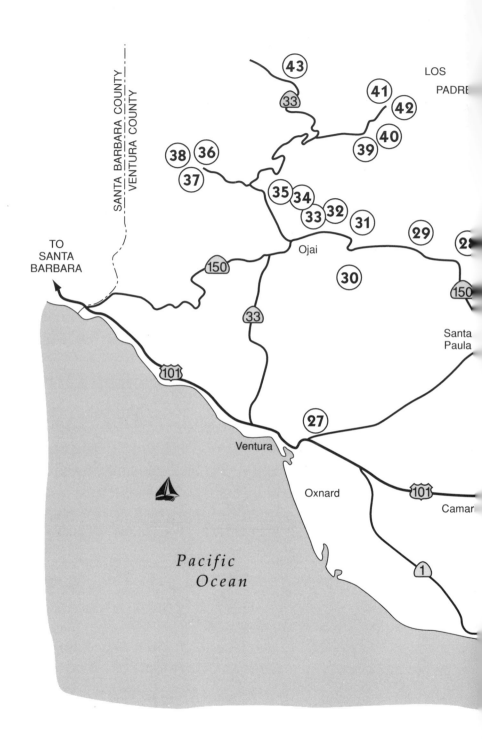

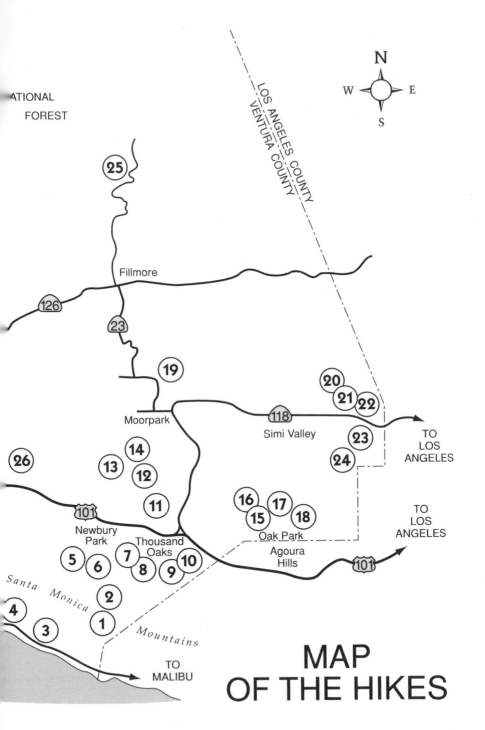

MAP
OF THE HIKES

Hike 1
Grotto Trail
Circle X Ranch

Hiking distance: 3.5 miles round trip
Hiking time: 2 hours
Elevation gain: 650 feet
Maps: Trail Map of the Santa Monica Mountains West
       U.S.G.S. Triunfo Pass

Summary of hike: The Grotto Trail is located in the 1,600-acre Circle X Ranch bordering Point Mugu State Park. Once a Boy Scout Wilderness Retreat, the Circle X Ranch is now a national park and recreation area. The Grotto is a maze of large, volcanic boulders in a sheer, narrow gorge formed from landslides. The West Fork of Arroyo Sequit flows through the caves and caverns of The Grotto, creating cascades and pools.

Driving directions: From the Pacific Coast Highway/Highway 1 and Las Posas Road in southeast Oxnard, drive 9 miles southbound on PCH to Yerba Buena Road and turn left. Continue 5.3 miles to the Circle X Ranger Station on the right. Park by the ranger station, or drive 0.1 mile downhill to the lower parking lot.
    Heading northbound on the Pacific Coast Highway, Yerba Buena Road is one mile northwest of the Los Angeles/Ventura County line.

Hiking directions: Follow the road a short distance downhill to the group campground and posted Grotto Trail on the left. Continue downhill, crossing the West Fork of Arroyo Sequit. At 0.4 miles, the trail recrosses the creek at the 30-foot waterfall. After crossing, the trail curves left, traversing a grassy ridge. Descend to the canyon floor where the trail joins the Happy Hollow Campground Road at 1.2 miles. Follow the road to the left into a primitive campground and cross the creek, picking up the posted Grotto Trail again. Head downstream to a bridge that crosses the creek into the Happy Hollow Campground. Instead of crossing the bridge, continue straight ahead and cross the creek by a pumphouse. Follow the creek a few hundred feet to The Grotto.

After exploring The Grotto, return to the bridge accessing the campground. Walk through the campground to the road and bear to the right. Follow the winding road, and rejoin the Grotto Trail on the left. Retrace your steps to the parking lot.

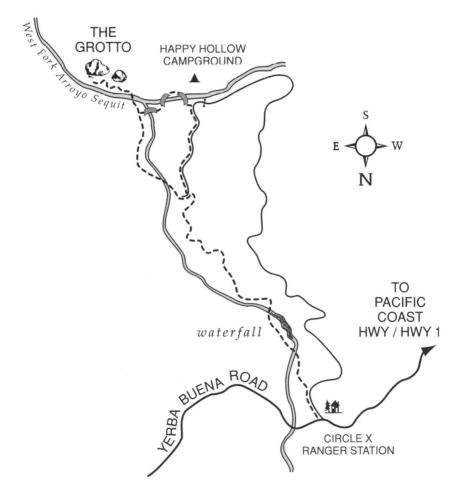

GROTTO TRAIL

Hike 2
Mishe Mokwa Trail
Circle X Ranch

Hiking distance: 6 mile loop
Hiking time: 3 hours
Elevation gain: 1,100 feet
Maps: Trail Map of the Santa Monica Mountains West
U.S.G.S. Triunfo Pass and Newbury Park

Summary of hike: The Mishe Mokwa Trail follows Carlisle Canyon past weathered red volcanic formations. There are views of the sculpted caves and crevices of Echo Cliffs and a forested streamside picnic area by a huge, split boulder known as Split Rock. The return route on the Backbone Trail leads to Inspiration Point and Sandstone Peak, the highest point in the Santa Monica Mountains. Both points overlook the Pacific Ocean, the Channel Islands, and the surrounding mountains.

Driving directions: From the Pacific Coast Highway/Highway 1 and Las Posas Road in southeast Oxnard, drive 9 miles southbound on PCH to Yerba Buena Road and turn left. Continue 6.3 miles (one mile past the ranger station) to the Backbone Trailhead parking lot on the left.

Heading northbound on Pacific Coast Highway, Yerba Buena Road is one mile northwest of the Los Angeles/Ventura County line.

Hiking directions: Take the Backbone Trail, a fire road, uphill to the north. At 0.3 miles, leave the road and take the signed Mishe Mokwa Connector Trail straight ahead. Continue 0.2 miles to a junction with the Mishe Mokwa Trail and take the left fork. The trail contours along Boney Mountain on the western edge of Carlisle Canyon. At 1.4 miles, Balanced Rock can be seen on the opposite side of the canyon. From here, the trail descends into the canyon to Split Rock and the picnic area.

Take the trail across the stream, heading out of the canyon, to another stream crossing by sculptured volcanic rocks. Parallel the stream to a signed junction. Take the left fork, the Backbone Trail, curving uphill towards Inspiration Point. A short side path leads up to the overlook. Continue east on the Backbone Trail to another junction. This side trail switchbacks up to the 360-degree views at Sandstone Peak. From the junction, it is 0.8 miles downhill back to the Mishe Mokwa Trail, completing the loop.

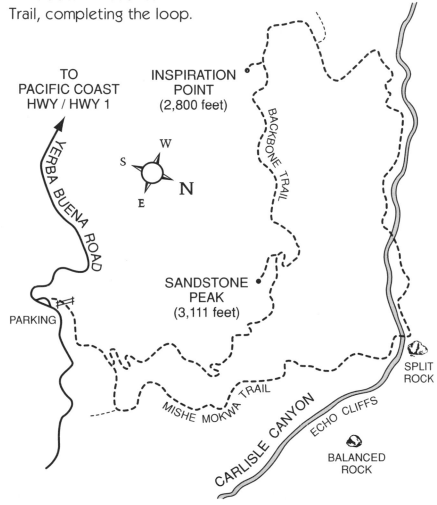

MISHE MOKWA TRAIL

Hike 3
Scenic and Overlook Trails Loop
Point Mugu State Park

Hiking distance: 2.5 miles round trip
Hiking time: 1 hour
Elevation gain: 900 feet
Maps: Trail Map of the Santa Monica Mountains West
U.S.G.S. Point Mugu

Summary of hike: The Scenic and Overlook Trails are located on the ocean side of Point Mugu State Park. The trail follows the ridge separating Big Sycamore Canyon from La Jolla Canyon. This short but beautiful hike climbs up the chaparral-covered ridge to several panoramic overlooks of the Pacific Ocean.

Driving directions: From the Pacific Coast Highway/Highway 1 and Las Posas Road in southeast Oxnard, drive 5.8 miles southbound on PCH to the Big Sycamore Canyon entrance on the left. Turn left and park in the day-use pay parking lot 0.1 mile ahead on the left. There is free parking in pullouts along PCH.
Heading northbound on Pacific Coast Highway, the Big Sycamore Canyon entrance is 4 miles northwest of the Los Angeles/Ventura County line.

Hiking directions: From the parking area, walk up the road past the campground to the Big Sycamore Canyon trailhead gate. Continue up the unpaved road about 50 yards to the signed junction with the Scenic Trail. Take the trail to the left (west) across a creekbed and up wooden steps. The trail steadily gains elevation up an open, grassy hillside. At the top of the hill is a trail split. The left fork leads a short distance to an ocean overlook. Continue up the hill to several more viewpoints. Return back to the junction, and head north to a junction with the Overlook Trail. Take this service road downhill to the right, winding 0.9 miles back to the Big Sycamore Canyon floor. Near the bottom, a series of five gentle switchbacks lead to the junction. Take the canyon trail to the right, leading 0.4 miles back to the trailhead gate.

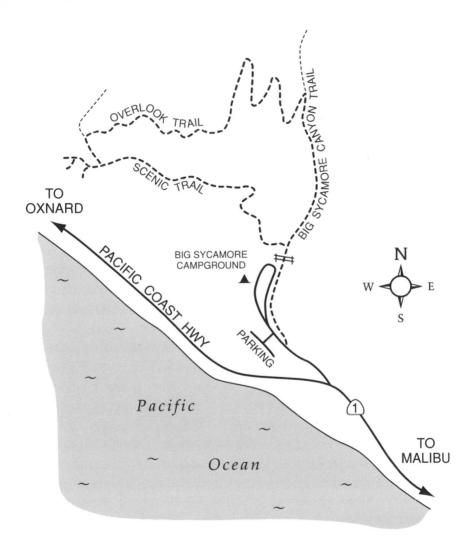

SCENIC AND OVERLOOK TRAILS LOOP

Hike 4
La Jolla Valley Loop from La Jolla Canyon
Point Mugu State Park

Hiking distance: 6 miles round trip
Hiking time: 3 hours
Elevation gain: 750 feet
Maps: Trail Map of the Santa Monica Mountains West
U.S.G.S. Point Mugu

Summary of hike: The La Jolla Canyon and La Jolla Valley Loop Trail have an assortment of highlights. The trail enters a narrow, steep gorge following a perennial stream to a 20-foot waterfall and pool. It crosses broad meadows with spectacular views of La Jolla Peak, Mugu Peak, and Laguna Peak. There is a coastal overlook and a pond by a picnic area.

Driving directions: From the Pacific Coast Highway/Highway 1 and Las Posas Road in southeast Oxnard, drive 4.2 miles southbound on PCH to the La Jolla Canyon entrance on the left. Turn left and park in the trailhead parking lot.
Heading northbound on the Pacific Coast Highway, the La Jolla Canyon entrance is 6 miles northwest of the Los Angeles/Ventura County line.

Hiking directions: From the parking lot and the Ray Miller Trailhead, head north up La Jolla Canyon. The trail crosses a stream at 0.4 miles and recrosses the stream a short distance ahead. The second crossing faces a beautiful waterfall and pool. Continue along the east side of the canyon, passing large sandstone rocks and caves. At a gorge, the trail sharply doubles back to the right, leading up the side of the canyon. At 1.2 miles, take the left fork towards Mugu Peak. Cross the stream and head southwest to a ridge above La Jolla Canyon and the ocean. The trail levels out and passes two trail junctions. Stay to the right both times, heading north across the rolling grassland. At 2.7 miles the trail joins the wide La Jolla Valley Loop Trail—head to the right. As you near the mountains of La Jolla Canyon, take the first cutoff trail to the right, leading past the pond and rejoining the La Jolla Canyon Trail. Head to the right, two miles down canyon, returning to the trailhead.

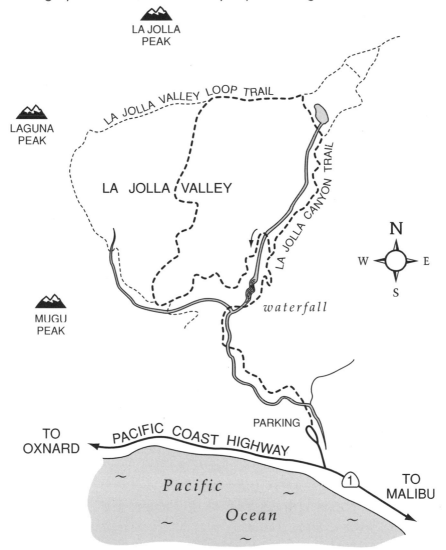

LA JOLLA VALLEY LOOP

Hike 5
Big Sycamore Canyon Trail
Point Mugu State Park

Hiking distance: 8.4 miles one-way (car shuttle)
Hiking time: 3 hours
Elevation loss: 900 feet
Maps: Trail Map of the Santa Monica Mountains West
U.S.G.S. Newbury Park, Camarillo, and Point Mugu

Summary of hike: The Big Sycamore Canyon Trail is a one-way mountains-to-the-sea journey through the heart of Point Mugu State Park. The hike is on a service road that parallels a stream through a deep, wooded canyon beneath large trees.

Driving directions: Leave a shuttle car in the parking lot where the hike ends—follow the driving directions to Hike 3.
  To the trailhead: Return 5.8 miles back to Las Posas Road and drive 2.9 miles north to Hueneme Road—turn right. Continue one mile to West Potrero Road and turn right. Drive 6.6 miles (West Potrero Road becomes Lynn Road) to Reino Road and turn right. One block ahead is Potrero Road. Turn right and drive a half mile to the Point Mugu State Park parking lot on the left.

Hiking directions: Hike south along the service road past the Satwiwa Culture Center, entering Point Mugu State Park at 0.4 miles. At 0.6 miles is a junction with the Boney Mountain Trail on the left (Hike 6). Begin the winding descent on the paved road to the canyon floor. The trail crosses a wooden bridge over the creek to the Hidden Pond Trail junction on the right. This is an excellent single track alternative trail that rejoins the Big Sycamore Canyon Trail 1.7 miles down canyon. On the alternative trail, there is a split at 2.2 miles. Take the left fork to the Sycamore Camping and Picnic Area. At 3 miles is a signed "beach" path on the right. This is where the alternative trail rejoins the service road. Just past the junction is the Danielson

Ranch. Past the ranch, the trail is unpaved. Continue south down the forested canyon, past the Backbone Trail and the Overlook Trail (Hike 3) to the gate. From the gate, a paved road leads back to the shuttle car.

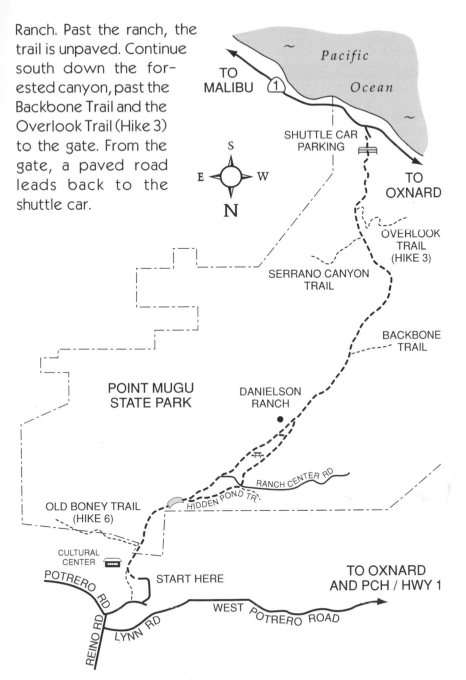

BIG SYCAMORE CANYON

Hike 6
Old Boney Trail to Sycamore Canyon Falls
Point Mugu State Park

Hiking distance: 3 miles round trip
Hiking time: 1.5 hours
Elevation gain: 350 feet
Maps: Trail Map of the Santa Monica Mountains West
      U.S.G.S. Newbury Park

Summary of hike: The Old Boney Trail leads to a multi-layered waterfall, unofficially named Sycamore Canyon Falls, at the western edge of the Santa Monica Mountains. The waterfall is surrounded by steep sandstone rock walls, lush vegetation, and small pools in the shade of a dense sycamore, bay, and oak forest. The hike begins in the Rancho Sierra Vista/Satwiwa area, a Native American Indian and early ranching site.

Driving directions: From Highway 101/Ventura Freeway in Newbury Park, exit on Wendy Drive. Drive 2.7 miles south to Potrero Road and turn right. Continue one mile, bearing left on Reino Road, to the Rancho Sierra Vista/Satwiwa and Point Mugu State Park parking lot on the left, across from Pinehill Road.

Hiking directions: From the parking lot, hike up the service road past the Satwiwa Native American Indian Cultural Center, entering Point Mugu State Park. As you approach the ridge overlooking Big Sycamore Canyon, take the signed Old Boney Trail to the left along the brink of the canyon. Climb a short hill, passing the Satwiwa Loop Trail on the left, and continue around a ridge to a trail split. Take the right fork, descending down to the forested canyon floor. Stay on the main trail, and cross the streambed where the trail switchbacks sharply to the right. Instead of taking this horseshoe turn to the right, bear to the left, taking the footpath 100 yards to a stream crossing and the waterfall. After enjoying the falls, return along the same trail.

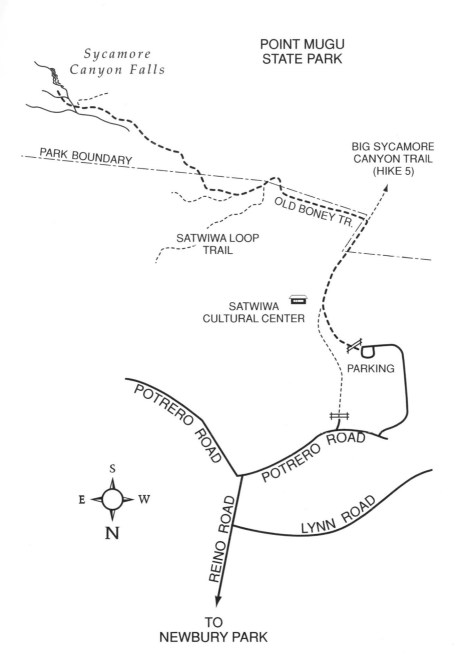

Sycamore Canyon Falls

POINT MUGU
STATE PARK

BIG SYCAMORE
CANYON TRAIL
(HIKE 5)

PARK BOUNDARY

OLD BONEY TR.

SATWIWA LOOP
TRAIL

SATWIWA
CULTURAL CENTER

PARKING

POTRERO ROAD

POTRERO ROAD

S

E — W

N

REINO ROAD

LYNN ROAD

TO
NEWBURY PARK

OLD BONEY TRAIL

Hike 7
Oak Creek Canyon
Los Robles Trail System

Hiking distance: 0.8 mile loop or 1.5 miles round trip
Hiking time: 30 to 45 minutes
Elevation gain: 100 feet
Maps: Los Robles Trail to Lake Sherwood map
      U.S.G.S. Newbury Park

Summary of hike: The first quarter mile of this hike is a gentle meander through an oak woodland along the Oak Creek Canyon Whole Access Trail. This portion of the hike has learning stations and a guide wire to assist the blind to the stations. The text at each station is written in English and Braille, describing the immediate surroundings through touch, smell, and sound. Beyond the Whole Access Trail, the trail loops through chaparral-covered hills, accessing a network of well-established trails in the Los Robles Trail System.

Driving directions: From Highway 101/Ventura Freeway in Thousand Oaks, exit on Moorpark Road. Drive 0.5 miles south to Greenmeadow Avenue—turn right. Continue 0.4 miles to the road's end and the trailhead parking lot at the Arts Council Center.

Hiking directions: From the parking lot, walk to the left (south) past the kiosk and restrooms. The trail begins in the forested canopy along a wooden fence. At the end of the quarter-mile Whole Access Trail, pass through the fence to the Oak Creek Canyon Loop. A short distance ahead is a junction. The right fork connects to the Los Robles Trail. Take the left fork, looping back to the north. At 3/4 mile, the trail connects with Greenmeadow Avenue. The parking lot is a short distance along the road to the left for a 0.8-mile loop. For a 1.5-mile hike, retrace your steps to the trailhead. You may also extend the hike on the Los Robles Trail (Hike 8).

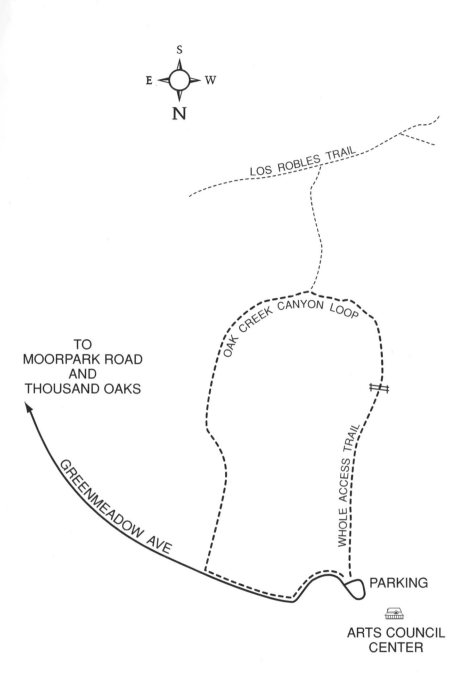

OAK CREEK CANYON

Hike 8
Los Padres—Los Robles Loop
Los Robles Trail System

Hiking distance: 3.5 mile loop
Hiking time: 1.5 hours
Elevation gain: 400 feet
Maps: Los Robles Trail to Lake Sherwood map
        U.S.G.S. Newbury Park

Summary of hike: The Los Padres Trail winds through an oak forest with a seasonal stream before joining the main Los Robles Trail. The main trail traverses an open meadow with unobstructed views of Hidden Valley and the Conejo Valley.

Driving directions: From Highway 101/Ventura Freeway in Thousand Oaks, exit on Moorpark Road. Drive 0.4 miles south to Los Padres Drive and turn left. Continue 100 yards and park by the trailhead gate on the right, located across the street from Woodlet Way.

Hiking directions: Hike south past the Los Padres Trailhead sign and gate through the oak forest along the trail. The trail parallels, then crosses, a seasonal stream. After crossing, begin a gradual but steady ascent from the canyon floor to the junction with the Los Robles Trail. Take the wide, signed trail to the right, continuing uphill to a junction at the top of the hill by a bench above the valley. Bear to the right on the Los Robles Trail West. In a quarter mile is a junction with the Scenic Overlook Loop on the right. Take this short trail through the open meadow overlooking Thousand Oaks and the Conejo Valley. After rejoining the Los Robles Trail, take the path downhill to the right. At the bottom are two trail splits. Bear to the right each time, following the signs to Moorpark Road. The trail exits at Moorpark Road. Walk one block and turn right at Los Padres Drive, returning to the trailhead.

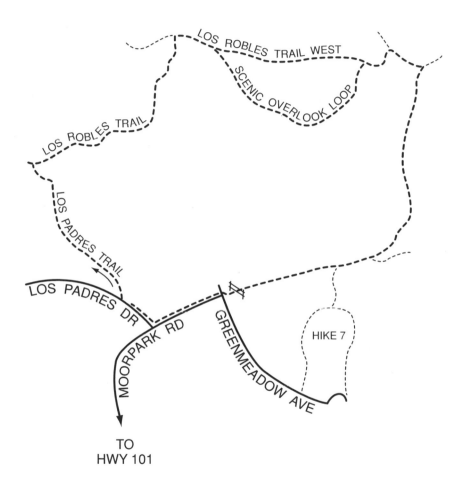

LOS PADRES–LOS ROBLES LOOP

Hike 9
White Horse Canyon Trail
Los Robles Trail System

Hiking distance: 3.5 mile loop
Hiking time: 1.5 hours
Elevation gain: 500 feet
Maps: Los Robles Trail to Lake Sherwood map
U.S.G.S. Thousand Oaks

Summary of hike: The White Horse Canyon Trail loops around the rolling, chaparral-covered foothills to a ridge overlooking Westlake Village and Thousand Oaks. There is an overlook with a panoramic view of Lake Sherwood and the Santa Monica Mountains.

Driving directions: From Highway 101/Ventura Freeway in Thousand Oaks, exit on Westlake Boulevard. Drive 1.8 miles south to East Potrero Road and turn right. Continue 0.5 miles and park on the right across from the Foxfield Riding Club, just beyond the bridge over Potrero Valley Creek.

Hiking directions: From the parking area, the trailhead and kiosk are across the creekbed to the north. Head up the hill, past the homes on the right, to a fire road. The fire road leads to a junction. The left fork is a short side trip to a scenic overlook of Lake Sherwood. Back at the junction, take the north fork 0.5 miles to another junction with the White Horse Canyon Trail on the left. This footpath loops around the back side of the canyon before rejoining the fire road. Take the road to the right uphill a short distance to a junction with the Conejo Crest Trail on the left. Head left along the ridge as it descends back down to Potrero Valley Creek. Cross the creekbed into the park. Take the park path to the right, leading back to the parking area.

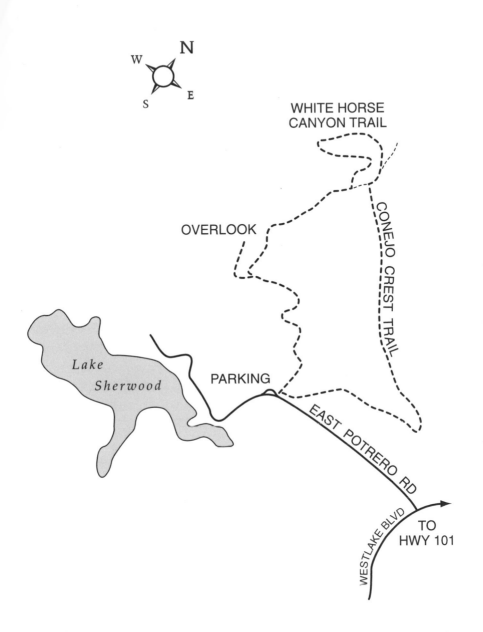

WHITE HORSE CANYON

Hike 10
Triunfo Canyon Trail
Los Robles Trail System

Hiking distance: 2.5 mile loop
Hiking time: 1 hour
Elevation gain: 400 feet
Maps: Los Robles Trail to Lake Sherwood map
U.S.G.S. Thousand Oaks

Summary of hike: The Triunfo Canyon Trail is part of the open space area near Westlake Village. The hike follows Triunfo Canyon to rolling grasslands with several wide open vistas of Westlake Village, the Conejo Valley, Lake Sherwood, and the Santa Monica Mountains. Part of the hike follows a short segment of the Los Robles Trail.

Driving directions: From Highway 101/Ventura Freeway in Thousand Oaks, exit on Hampshire Road. Drive 0.6 miles south to Triunfo Canyon Road and turn right. Continue 0.5 miles to Tamarack Street and turn right. The trailhead is 0.2 miles ahead in the parking lot at the north end of Triunfo Community Park.

Hiking directions: From the parking lot, head northwest on the signed trail past the kiosk. The trail gradually climbs along the contour of Triunfo Canyon to the ridgeline. Near the top, a short series of steep switchbacks lead to a bench. From the bench are great views of the valley below. The trail then levels out to a junction with the Los Robles Trail—go to the left. Thirty feet ahead is a ridge with views of the mountains and another junction. Take the signed "Los Robles Trail South" to the left to a third trail split. Proceed downhill on the left fork. The trail ends at Brookview Avenue. Walk through the neighborhood one block to Stonesgate Street. Go to the left and proceed one block to Aranmoor Avenue. Go left again, returning to the park. The park path heads left, leading back to the parking lot.

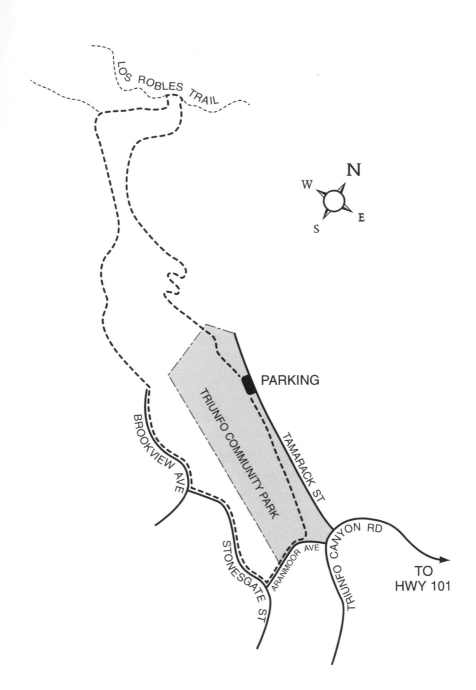

TRIUNFO CANYON TRAIL

Hike 11
Conejo Valley Botanic Garden

Hiking distance: 1.5 miles round trip
Hiking time: 1 hour
Elevation gain: 100 feet
Maps: Conejo Valley Botanic Garden map

Summary of hike: The Conejo Valley Botanic Garden in Thousand Oaks encompasses 33 acres. The garden's meandering paths lead past native plants and fruit trees and include sections of desert, Mediterranean, herb, and butterfly gardens. From the gardens, a nature trail follows a creek in a natural oak and willow-lined canyon.

Driving directions: From Highway 101/Ventura Freeway in Thousand Oaks, exit on Lynn Road. Head 0.6 miles north to Gainsborough Road and turn right. Continue 0.5 miles to the Conejo Valley Botanic Garden entrance and turn right. The parking lot is 0.2 miles ahead on the left.

Hiking directions: From the parking lot, walk to the end of the road to the botanic garden entrance. Hike up the pathway into Conejo Community Park. A sign directs you to the right into the garden to an information kiosk and trail junction. Take the left fork on the upper trail to another junction. Steps lead straight ahead to benches and overlooks. Many interconnecting trails lead to various overlooks. There are numerous garden paths and a nature trail that descends into a forested canyon to a junction by the creek. The left fork leads deeper into the canyon and crosses a wooden bridge over the creek. The right fork crosses the creek. In both cases, you must reverse your route to return. After enjoying the gardens, return to the parking lot.

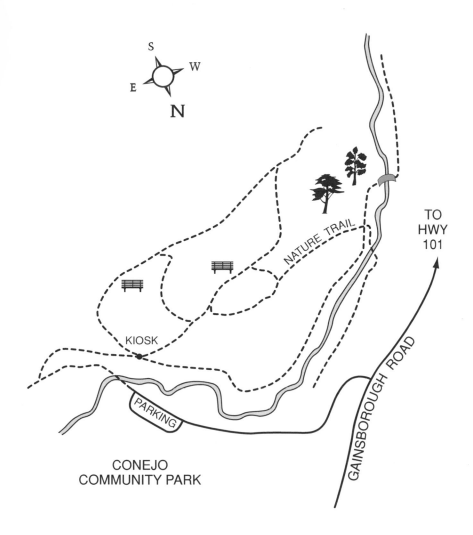

CONEJO VALLEY
BOTANIC GARDEN

Hike 12
Paradise Falls
Wildwood Park

Hiking distance: 3 miles round trip
Hiking time: 1.5 hours
Elevation gain: 400 feet
Maps: Wildwood Park Trail Guide
U.S.G.S. Newbury Park

Summary of hike: Paradise Falls, a dramatic, 70-foot water-fall, plunges down over a wall of volcanic rock into a pool below (back cover photo). The hike to Paradise Falls loops through Wildwood Park. The return hike follows Indian Creek through Wildwood Canyon. There are two creek crossings and two smaller waterfalls.

Driving directions: From Highway 101/Ventura Freeway in Thousand Oaks, exit on Lynn Road, and drive 2.5 miles north to Avenida de los Arboles. Turn left and continue 0.9 miles to the end of the road at Big Sky Drive. Loop around the center median, and park in the trailhead parking lot on the right.

Hiking directions: Take the trail to the east, away from the mountains. Descend wooden steps to the Moonridge and Indian Creek Trail junction. Take the Moonridge Trail along the west ridge of Wildwood Canyon. Switchbacks lead down into the canyon and across a wooden bridge. Proceed to a service road. After crossing, stay on the Moonridge Trail along the hilly contours to another junction. Take the signed left fork towards Paradise Falls, crossing a small ravine to the Teepee Overlook Trail, a service road. Head left to Teepee Overlook. Proceed along the road for about 100 years into the canyon to a signed junction. Take the left trail down the steps to Paradise Falls.

After exploring the area around the falls and pool, return up the steps. Take the Wildwood Canyon Trail to the right past the brink of the falls. You will pass Little Falls and a picnic area as the trail parallels Indian Creek. Cross the creek on a wooden bridge, and take the signed Indian Creek Trail up the canyon to the left. Cross the creek again and ascend the hill to the top. The left fork leads back to the parking lot.

Paradise Falls

Little Falls

TEEPEE OVERLOOK TR.

SERVICE ROADS

INDIAN CREEK TR.

MOONRIDGE TRAIL

HIKES 13 & 14

W
S
N
E

BIG SKY DR

PARKING

AVENIDA DE LOS ARBOLES

TO LYNN ROAD

PARADISE FALLS

Hike 13
Lizard Rock
Wildwood Park

Hiking distance: 3 miles round trip
Hiking time: 1.5 hours
Elevation gain: 150 feet
Maps: Wildwood Park Trail Guide
U.S.G.S. Newbury Park

Summary of hike: The hike to Lizard Rock parallels Mountclef Ridge, a serrated, volcanic rock outcropping. From the Lizard Rock formation are panoramic views of the surrounding mountains and valleys. The return route follows the edge of the cliffs above Wildwood Canyon.

Driving directions: From Highway 101/Ventura Freeway in Thousand Oaks, exit on Lynn Road and drive 2.5 miles north to Avenida de los Arboles. Turn left and continue 0.9 miles to the end of the road at Big Sky Drive. Loop around the center median, and park in the trailhead parking lot on the right.

Hiking directions: Head west past the trailhead information board and up a short hill. Drop down over the hill to a service road. Follow the road 70 yards to the Mesa Trail veering off to the right. Take the Mesa Trail across the grasslands, passing the Santa Rosa Trail (Hike 14) and the Teepee Overlook Trail to a posted trail split. Take the right fork, the Box Canyon Trail, to a knoll. From the knoll, take the left path to the Lizard Rock Trail. Continue along the Lizard Rock Trail to the right. Ascend a short, steep hill to the top of the rock. The trail loops around and rejoins the trail coming up. Retrace your steps to the signed Stagecoach Bluff Trail. Take this trail to the right along the cliff edge overlooking Wildwood Canyon. The trail ends at a junction with the Teepee Overlook Trail. Turn left, rejoining the Mesa Trail 100 yards ahead. Return to the trailhead on the right.

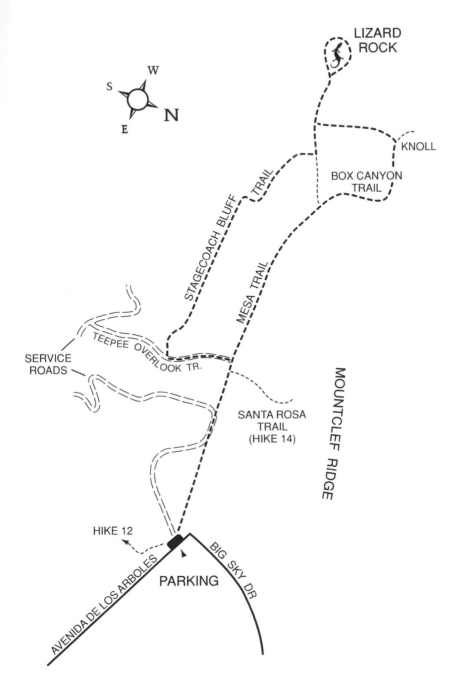

LIZARD ROCK

Hike 14
Santa Rosa Trail
Wildwood Park

Hiking distance: 5 mile loop
Hiking time: 2.5 hours
Elevation gain: 400 feet
Maps: Wildwood Park Trail Guide
  U.S.G.S. Newbury Park

Summary of hike: The Santa Rosa Trail traverses Mountclef Ridge, a volcanic rock outcropping. From the summit of this rocky range are great views north across the Santa Rosa Valley to the Santa Susana and Topatopa Mountains and views to the south across the Conejo Valley to the Santa Monica Mountains.

Driving directions: From Highway 101/Ventura Freeway in Thousand Oaks, exit on Lynn Road and drive 2.5 miles north to Avenida de los Arboles. Turn left and continue 0.9 miles to the end of the road at Big Sky Drive. Loop around the center median, and park in the trailhead parking lot on the right.

Hiking directions: Hike west past the trailhead kiosk and up a short hill to a trail split. Bear to the right, passing a gate on the Mesa Trail, to another trail junction 100 yards ahead. Take the Santa Rosa Trail to the right, and head north towards the prominent Mountclef Ridge. The trail traverses the hillside to the east and switchbacks up to the saddle of the Mountclef Ridge summit. Topping the slope, take the right fork, staying on the Santa Rosa Trail along the contour of the cliff's ridge. A short distance ahead, the trail drops down along the northern slope. Continue east, past the junction with the Wildwood Avenue access trail, to a service road. Take the road to the right to a housing development. Cross the road and continue straight ahead on the signed Lower Butte Trail. Watch for a footpath on the right leading up to a saddle and over the ridge to the trail's end at Wildwood Avenue. Go left and walk 0.4 miles downhill on the sidewalk to a footpath on the right across from Sundance Street. Take the path, following a canal into Wildflower Playfield Park, to Avenida de los Arboles. Complete the loop, returning to the parking lot on the right.

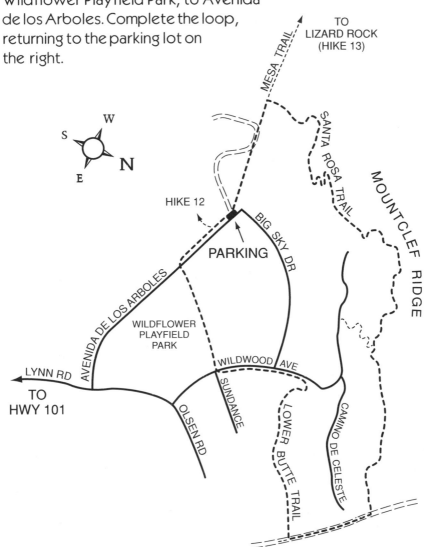

SANTA ROSA TRAIL

Hike 15
Oak Canyon Community Park
Nature Trail

Hiking distance: 1.6 miles round trip
Hiking time: 45 minutes
Elevation gain: 100 feet

Summary of hike: Oak Canyon Community Park is a beautiful, 60-acre park with sandstone cliffs and a year-round creek. The park has a nature trail that loops through the oak forest, crossing several times over Medea Creek. Near the trailhead by Kanan Road is a beautiful, manmade waterfall cascading into a pond. Walking paths circle the pond.

Driving directions: From Highway 101/Ventura Freeway in Agoura Hills, exit on Kanan Road. Head north 3 miles to Hollytree Drive and turn right. Turn left 70 yards ahead into the Oak Canyon Community Park parking lot.

Hiking directions: From the parking lot, take the paved walking path north past the restrooms, playground, and covered picnic area. Follow the curving path up canyon on the east side of Medea Creek and the park road. Various side trails lead down into the oak tree canopy to the creek. The trail reaches nature trail station #8 at 0.4 miles. Take the footpath to the left, leading into the forest to Medea Creek. The trail begins down the canyon and crosses the creek three times. After the third crossing, by station #15, is a junction. The right fork is a quarter-mile side trip through chaparral to an archery range at the back of a small canyon. The left fork leads back to the pond and the trailhead. Several paths cross the creek to the parking lot, or you may circle around the pond.

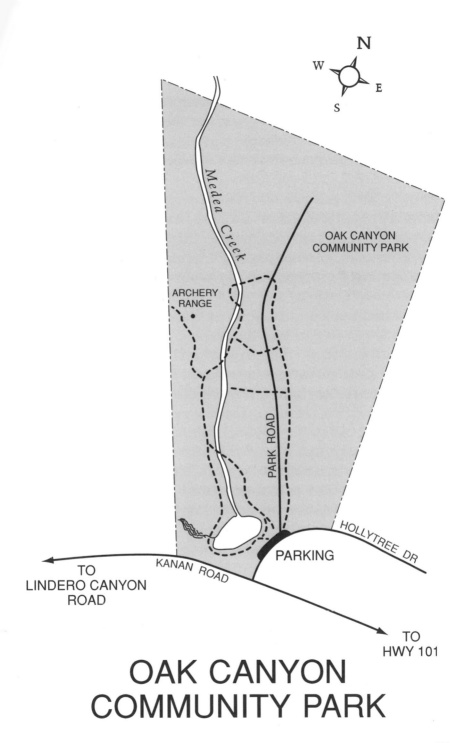

OAK CANYON
COMMUNITY PARK

Hike 16
China Flat Trail

Hiking distance: 4 mile loop
Hiking time: 2 hours
Elevation gain: 1,000 feet
Maps: Cheeseboro Canyon/Palo Comado Canyon Site map
  U.S.G.S. Thousand Oaks

Summary of hike: China Flat, the newest addition to the Cheeseboro Canyon/Palo Comado Canyon Site, sits beneath the shadows of Simi Peak, the highest peak in the Simi Hills. The China Flat Trail is a steep hike with awesome, panoramic views of Simi Valley, Oak Park, and Agoura Hills. From the top, the trail follows the southern perimeter of China Flat.

Driving directions: From Highway 101/Ventura Freeway in Westlake, exit on Lindero Canyon Road. Drive 4 miles north and park on Lindero Canyon Road by the China Flat Trailhead on the left. It is located between King James Court and Wembly Avenue.

Hiking directions: Hike north past the trailhead sign towards the mountains. Climb the short, steep hill to where a trail from King James Court merges with the main trail. Continue around the east side of a large sandstone outcropping. The trail levels out and heads east, following the contour of the mountain base, to an unsigned trail junction. Take the left fork north, heading uphill towards the ridge. Once over the ridge, the trail meets another unsigned junction. Take the left fork and head west. From here are views overlooking the canyon. Proceed uphill along the ridgeline to a flat area and trail junction. The right fork leads back towards Palo Comado and Cheeseboro Canyons. Take the left fork and descend to another junction. Again, take the left fork, winding downhill to a gate at King James Court. Leave the trail and walk one block on the sidewalk to Lindero Canyon Road. The trailhead is on the left.

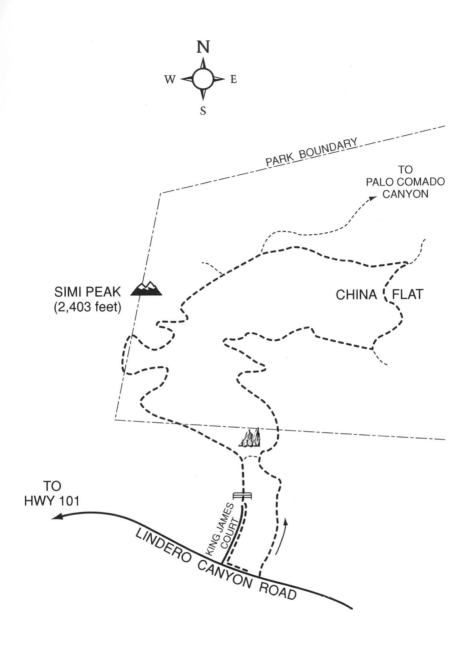

N
W E
S

PARK BOUNDARY

TO
PALO COMADO
CANYON

SIMI PEAK
(2,403 feet)

CHINA FLAT

TO
HWY 101

KING JAMES
COURT

LINDERO CANYON ROAD

CHINA FLAT TRAIL

Hike 17
Palo Comado Canyon

Hiking distance: 5 miles round trip
Hiking time: 2.5 hours
Elevation gain: 800 feet
Maps: Cheeseboro Canyon/Palo Comado Canyon Site map
U.S.G.S. Thousand Oaks and Calabasas

Summary of hike: Palo Comado Canyon lies adjacent to Cheeseboro Canyon about a mile to the west. Although not part of the Santa Monica Mountains, the canyons are part of the Santa Monica Mountains National Recreation Area. This hike heads up the undeveloped Palo Comado Canyon and crosses over into Cheeseboro Canyon. The trail parallels a stream through meadows, oak groves, and rock outcroppings.

Driving directions: From Highway 101/Ventura Freeway in Agoura Hills, exit on Kanan Road. Head north 2.2 miles to Sunnycrest Drive and turn right. Continue 0.8 miles to the "Public Open Space" sign on the right. Park along the curb.

Hiking directions: From the trailhead, hike east past the gate and up a short hill on the Sunnycrest Connector Trail. As you top the hill, the trail descends into Palo Comado Canyon. Cross the stream at the canyon floor to a junction with the Palo Comado Canyon Trail, an old ranch road. Head left, up the canyon through rolling grasslands and oak groves. At one mile the trail begins to climb out of the canyon, winding along the contours of the mountain. Near the head of the canyon the Palo Comado Canyon Trail curves left, heading to China Flat. There is an unmarked but distinct path leading sharply to the right at the beginning of this curve—the Old Sheep Corral Trail. Take this path uphill to a couple of ridges that overlook Cheeseboro Canyon. Descend into the canyon a short distance to the corral and a junction at Shephards' Flat. This is the turnaround spot.

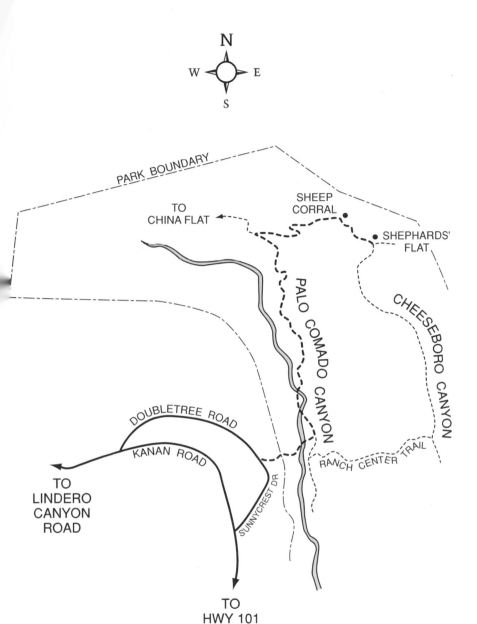

PALO COMADO CANYON

Hike 18
Cheeseboro Canyon

Hiking distance: 8.6 miles round trip
Hiking time: 4 hours
Elevation gain: 600 feet
Maps: Cheeseboro Canyon/Palo Comado Canyon Site map
U.S.G.S. Calabasas

Summary of hike: The hike through Cheeseboro Canyon follows along an abandoned ranch road. The trail rambles through a lush canopy of sycamore and oak trees and across rolling grasslands.

Driving directions: From Highway 101/Ventura Freeway in Agoura Hills, exit on Chesebro Road. Continue one block straight ahead, past the stop sign, to Palo Comado Canyon Road and turn left. Drive 0.3 miles to Chesebro Road and turn right. Continue 0.7 miles to Cheeseboro Canyon Road and turn right. The trailhead parking lot is 0.2 miles ahead.

Hiking directions: Take the service road east toward Cheeseboro Canyon to a road split. Bear left on the Cheeseboro Canyon Trail, heading into the canyon past the Modelo Trail and the Canyon View Trail. At 1.3 miles is a junction with the Baleen Wall Trail. Take the left fork towards Sulphur Springs to another junction with the Modelo Trail on the left. Proceed a short distance on the main trail to a signed trail junction. Leave the main trail, branching to the left on the Sulphur Springs Trail. As you near Sulphur Springs, the white, jagged cliffs of the Baleen Wall can be seen towering on the cliffs to the east. At 3.5 miles, the canyon and trail both narrow as the smell of sulphur becomes stronger. At the head of the canyon is a three-way junction at Shephards' Flat, the turnaround point. Return back to the Modelo Trail junction. Take the Modelo Trail along the western ridge of the canyon back to the trailhead.

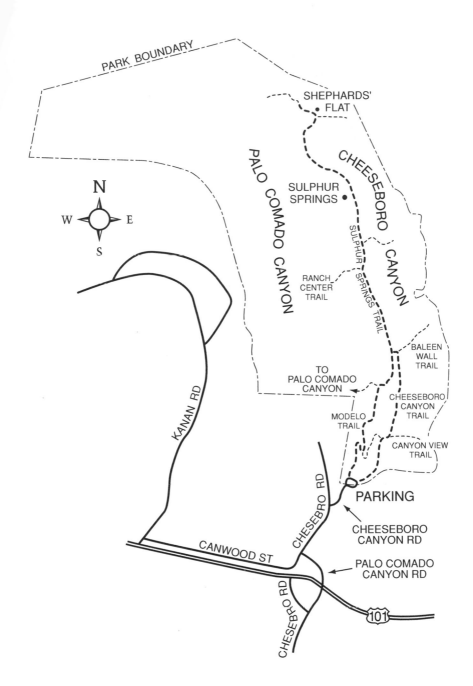

CHEESEBORO CANYON

Hike 19
Happy Camp Canyon

Hiking distance: 10 miles round trip
Hiking time: 4 hours
Elevation gain: 800 feet
Maps: U.S.G.S. Simi Valley West

Summary of hike: Happy Camp Canyon Park, north of Moorpark in the Santa Susana Mountains, was once part of a cattle ranch. The canyon is sheltered by Oak Ridge to the north and Big Mountain to the south. The Happy Camp Trail follows an abandoned ranch road through a shady, forested canyon.

Driving directions: From the town of Moorpark, take Moorpark Avenue (Highway 23) 2.5 miles north to a sharp left bend in the road. Continue straight ahead 30 yards on Happy Camp Road to Broadway Street and turn right. Drive 0.3 miles to the Happy Camp Canyon parking lot at the road's end.

Hiking directions: Overlooking the valley, the trail heads downhill past the trailhead sign. Cross the hillside to the grassy valley floor, joining the old ranch road at one mile. Turn left up canyon a quarter mile to the Happy Camp Canyon Nature Trail kiosk. One hundred yards beyond the kiosk is a trail split. The right fork heads up Big Mountain, an alternative return route. Take the left fork, curving east into the shady canyon, parallel to and across the stream. At 3.5 miles is the first of several road forks. The left (north) forks are powerline maintenance roads. Take the right fork each time, staying in the canyon. At 4.5 miles, the trail passes a gate, entering an oak grove with picnic tables and horse corrals. This is the turnaround spot.

To make a loop, continue east to a junction. Take the steep, half-mile trail to the right, gaining 600 feet to the ridge of Big Mountain. Return along the ridge road to the right, descending to the valley floor and completing the loop near the kiosk.

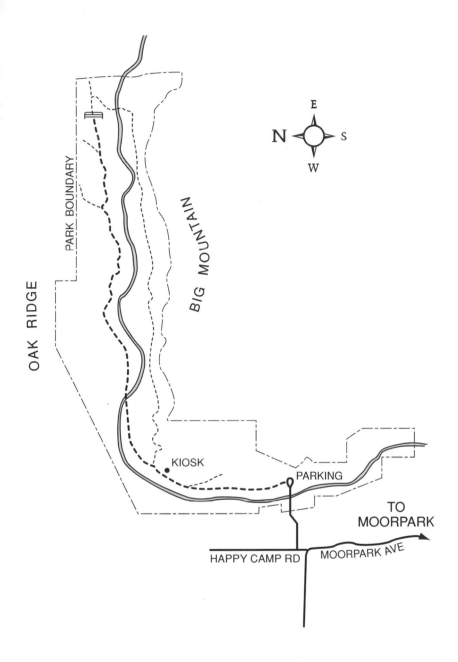

HAPPY CAMP CANYON

Hike 20
Chumash Trail
Rocky Peak Park

Hiking distance: 5 miles round trip
Hiking time: 2.5 hours
Elevation gain: 1,100 feet
Maps: U.S.G.S. Simi Valley East

Summary of hike: The Chumash Trail ascends the Santa Susana Mountains in Rocky Peak Park north of Simi Valley. The trail overlooks Simi Valley, the Simi Hills, the Santa Susana Mountains, Las Llajas Canyon, and Blind Canyon. There are beautiful vistas from both Hamilton Saddle and the Rocky Peak Trail junction.

Driving directions: From Highway 118/Ronald Reagan Freeway in Simi Valley, exit on Yosemite Avenue. Drive 0.4 miles north to Flanagan Drive and turn right. Continue 0.8 miles to the trailhead at the end of the road.

Hiking directions: The trail heads north, past the kiosk, along the rolling hills and grassy meadows. The trail climbs steadily as you round the hillside to the first overlook of the Simi Hills to the south. From the overlook, the trail continues uphill, curving left around the next rolling hill. The trail passes sculpted sandstone formations. Arrow signposts are placed along the route. Continue to the east along the edge of the canyon to Hamilton Saddle. From the saddle, the trail sharply curves left (north), gaining elevation before leveling out again at Flat Rock. From Flat Rock, the trail begins its final ascent as it curves around the last ridge to the top. The trail ends at a junction with the Rocky Peak Trail at an elevation of 2,450 feet. Sixty yards to the left of the junction is a view to the east of Blind Canyon and to the west of Las Llajas Canyon. Reverse your route to return.

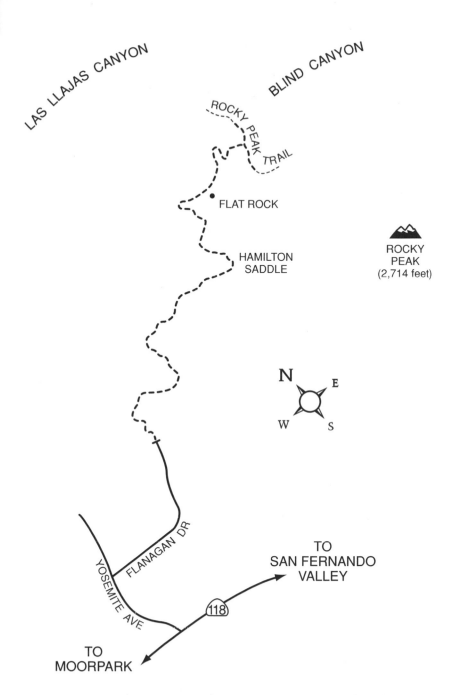

CHUMASH TRAIL

Hike 21
Hummingbird Trail
Rocky Peak Park

Hiking distance: 4.6 miles round trip
Hiking time: 2 hours
Elevation gain: 1,000 feet
Maps: U.S.G.S. Simi Valley East

Summary of hike: The Hummingbird Trail is located in the 5,000-acre Rocky Peak Park at the base of Rocky Peak in the Santa Susana Mountains. The trail climbs through open chaparral and up a canyon, passing stacks of giant sandstone boulders, sculpted caves, and dramatic rock outcroppings.

Driving directions: From Highway 118/Ronald Reagan Freeway in Simi Valley, exit on Kuehner Drive. Drive 0.3 miles north to the signed trailhead on the right. Park in one of the pullouts alongside the road. If full, additional parking is available just north of the freeway.

Hiking directions: From the parking pullouts and trailhead kiosk, head downhill to the north. The trail then U-turns southeast into the canyon to a defunct rock dam and Hummingbird Creek. Proceed past the dam into an oak grove and meadow. Once past the meadow, the trail crosses Hummingbird Creek and begins the ascent up the mountain through the chaparral. Switchbacks lead up to the sandstone caves and rock formations. After the cluster of rocks and caves, the trail levels out before the second ascent. With the aid of additional switchbacks, the climb is not difficult as it heads up the canyon. At the head of the canyon, the trail levels out and passes more rock formations. The trail ends at a junction with the Rocky Peak Trail (Hike 22). Return to the trailhead by retracing your steps.

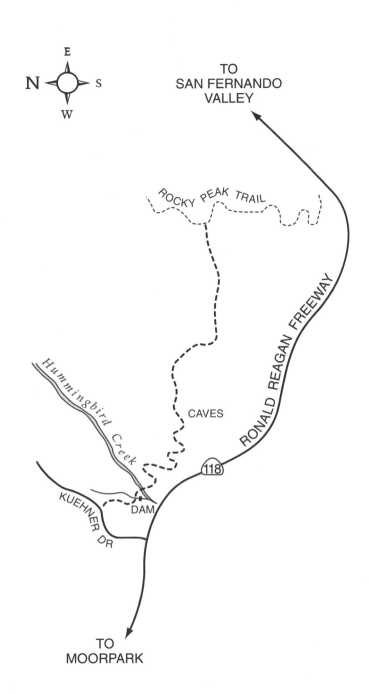

HUMMINGBIRD TRAIL

Hike 22
Rocky Peak Trail
Rocky Peak Park

Hiking distance: 5 miles round trip
Hiking time: 2.5 hours
Elevation gain: 1,100 feet
Maps: U.S.G.S. Simi Valley East

Summary of hike: The Rocky Peak Trail is on the east side of Simi Valley by Santa Susana Pass. This uphill hike follows a winding fire road to Rocky Peak. From the peak are top-of-the-world views of the San Fernando Valley, Simi Valley, and the many peaks of the Los Padres National Forest. The trail is surrounded by dramatic sandstone formations and a continuous series of vista points with views in every direction.

Driving directions: From Highway 118/Ronald Reagan Freeway in Simi Valley, exit on Kuehner Drive. Drive 3 miles south to the Highway 118 East on-ramp. (Along the way, Kuehner Drive becomes Santa Susana Pass Road.) Turn left, crossing over the freeway, and park 0.1 mile ahead at the end of the road.

Hiking directions: Hike past the trailhead kiosk up a winding fire road to an unsigned trail split at 0.9 miles. Stay to the left on the main trail, hiking steadily uphill to a signed junction with the Hummingbird Trail on the left (Hike 21). Proceed straight ahead on the Rocky Peak Trail, which levels out. The winding trail offers alternating views of the San Fernando Valley to the east and Simi Valley to the west. At the base of the final ascent to the Rocky Peak Cutoff Trail is a singular, large oak tree. Begin the ascent, gaining 450 feet in a half mile, to the Rocky Peak Cutoff Trail. This is our turnaround spot.

If you wish to hike further, the trail takes off to the right across the plateau for a half mile to Rocky Peak. The last portion is a rock scramble to the peak. To return, reverse your route.

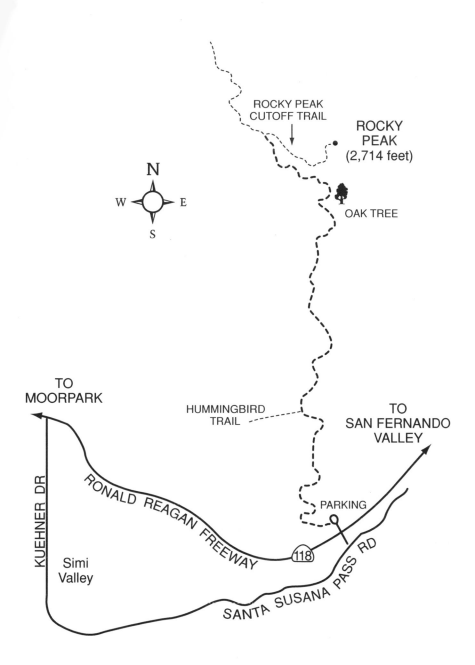

ROCKY PEAK TRAIL

Hike 23
Corriganville Park

Hiking distance: 2 miles round trip
Hiking time: 1 hour
Elevation gain: 100 feet
Maps: Rancho Simi Open Space: Corriganville Park
       U.S.G.S. Simi Valley East

Summary of hike: Corriganville Park, an old movie ranch, was the setting to about a thousand movie and television shows between 1937 and 1965. They include *The Lone Ranger, Gunsmoke, The Fugitive, Lassie, Mutiny on the Bounty, African Queen, How The West Was Won,* and *Fort Apache,* to name just a few. Old stone and concrete foundations from the sets still remain. The oak-shaded paths lead through the 225-acre park, passing prominent sandstone outcroppings, cliffs, caves, a stream, and Jungle Jim Lake.

Driving directions: From Highway 118/Ronald Reagan Freeway in Simi Valley, exit on Kuehner Drive. Drive 1.1 mile south to Smith Road and turn left. Continue 0.4 miles into Corriganville Park, and park on the left.

Hiking directions: From the far end of the parking lot, take the wide trail past the kiosk. The forested trail heads northeast up the draw past sculpted rock formations on the left. Cross a bridge to a junction. The left fork crosses a wooden bridge, passes a pool, and loops back for a short hike. Stay to the right to the next junction. Curve to the left and cross the stream to another junction. Both trails lead west back to the trailhead. The footpath to the right follows the northern edge of the park between the sandstone cliffs to a dynamic overlook and junction. Take the left fork, descending to the old movie sets. From the sets, cross the bridge back to the parking lot.

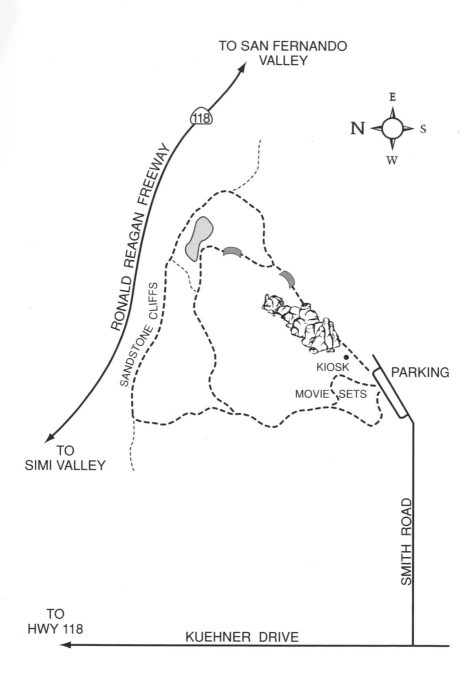

CORRIGANVILLE PARK

Hike 24
Sage Ranch Loop Trail

Hiking distance: 2.6 mile loop
Hiking time: 1.3 hours
Elevation gain: 300 feet
Maps: Santa Monica Mountains Conservancy: Sage Ranch Park
U.S.G.S. Calabasas

Summary of hike: Sage Ranch, sitting at 2,000 feet, has a garden-of-the-gods appearance. Located in the Simi Hills overlooking the valley, this 635-acre park is rich with world-class sandstone formations. The park boasts an endless display of unique boulders and outcrops. Sandstone Ridge, a long, steep, weathered formation with caves and natural sculptures, rises 300 feet from the trail. Beautiful carved boulders and eucalyptus trees fill the canyon section of this loop trail.

Driving directions: From Highway 118/Ronald Reagan Freeway in the San Fernando Valley, exit on Topanga Canyon Blvd. Drive south and turn right on Plummer Street. Continue 2.4 miles to Woolsey Canyon Road and turn right. (Along the way, Plummer Street becomes Valley Circle Boulevard and Lake Manor Drive.) Continue on Woolsey Canyon Road 2.4 miles to Black Canyon Road and turn right. The Sage Ranch parking lot is on the left 0.2 miles ahead.

From Highway 101/Ventura Freeway in the San Fernando Valley, exit on Valley Circle Boulevard. Drive north to Woolsey Canyon Road and turn left.

Hiking directions: From the parking lot, hike west up the park service road. Proceed through the gate, passing orange trees on both sides. At the top of the hill, next to sandstone formations, the trail leaves the paved road and takes the gravel road to the right (north). Continue past a meadow dotted with oak trees and through an enormous garden of sandstone rock formations. Watch for a short path on the right to a vista point overlooking Simi Valley. Back on the main trail, the trail parallels Sandstone Ridge before descending into the canyon. Once in the canyon, the trail curves back to the east past another series of large rock formations. Near the east end of the canyon is a trail split. Take the left fork, heading uphill and out of the canyon, back to the parking lot.

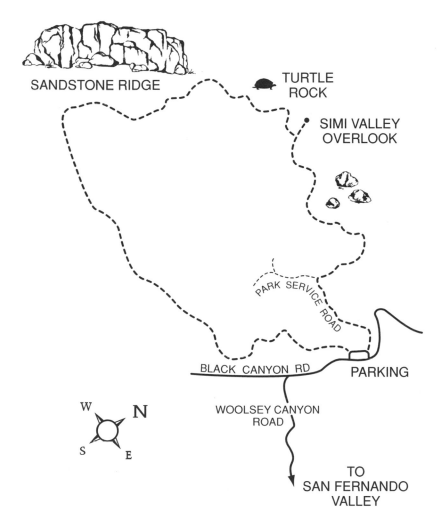

SANDSTONE RIDGE

TURTLE
ROCK

SIMI VALLEY
OVERLOOK

PARK SERVICE ROAD

BLACK CANYON RD

PARKING

W N S E

WOOLSEY CANYON
ROAD

TO
SAN FERNANDO
VALLEY

SAGE RANCH TRAIL

Hike 25
Tar Creek

Hiking distance: 4 miles round trip
Hiking time: 2 hours
Elevation gain: 700 feet
Maps: U.S.G.S. Fillmore

Summary of hike: Tar Creek is in the Sespe Condor Sanctuary, a reintroduction area for the California Condor. This hike is located in the Los Padres National Forest north of Fillmore. The well-defined but lightly used trail descends into a deep canyon to Tar Creek. Along Tar Creek is a grotto of sculptured, sandstone boulders with smooth, water-filled bowls and moss-covered rocks. There are pools, cascades, and waterfalls.

Driving directions: From the town of Fillmore, take A Street (Highway 23) one mile north to Goodenough Road. Turn right and continue 2.7 miles Squaw Flat Road on the right. It is marked as the Dough Flat turnoff. Turn right and drive 4.8 miles up the winding mountain road to the unsigned parking pullout on the left. It is located 1.5 miles beyond the Oak Flat Guard Station.

Hiking directions: From the parking area, take the wide path northwest past the metal gate. The trail winds around the mountainside with views of the canyon below and the surrounding mountains. As the trail begins its descent, the path narrows to a single track. At the final descent, the trail overlooks Tar Creek. Once at the creek, explore up and down the stream. There are more waterfalls and pools downstream, but the hike becomes demanding and technical. After enjoying the creek, return along the same path.

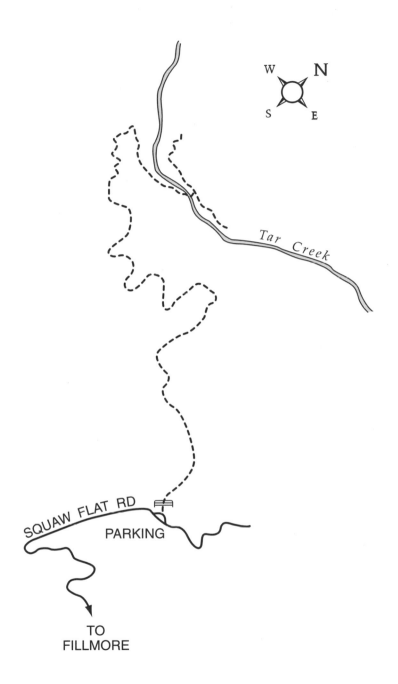

TAR CREEK

Hike 26
Mission Oaks Community Park Trail

Hiking distance: 2 miles round trip
Hiking time: 1 hour
Elevation gain: 100 feet
Maps: U.S.G.S. Camarillo

Summary of hike: The Mission Oaks Park Trail leads through a natural area with hills and canyons connecting Mission Oaks Park and Mission Verde Park. Mission Oaks Park is a developed park with baseball fields, tennis courts, and a picnic area. Mission Verde Park is a grassy hilltop flat overlooking the open space. The forested trail parallels a seasonal waterway.

Driving directions: From Highway 101/Ventura Freeway in Camarillo, take the Pleasant Valley Road/Santa Rosa Road exit. Drive 1.6 miles north to Oak Canyon Road and turn left. Continue 0.4 miles—crossing Mission Oaks Boulevard—to Mission Oaks Community Park. Park in the lot to the left near the tennis courts.

Hiking directions: From the parking lot, walk between the tennis courts and Mission Oaks Boulevard to the trailhead. The path leads downhill and crosses a wooden footbridge to a five-way junction. Continue straight ahead on the main path. After crossing a drainage creek, the trail curves to the right. A narrow side path leads to the left up the hill into Mission Verde Park. Return to the main trail, and continue north to a trail split. Take the left fork up the draw. Near the northwest corner of the park, the trail heads up a short hill to a junction. The left fork leads to Woodcreek Road. Take the right fork east across the head of the canyon. Descend back down into the canyon, completing the loop. Retrace your steps to the bridge and the five-way junction. Take the right fork through the tunnel under the road. The trail curves 0.4 miles through a wooded area and ends at Santa Rosa Road. Return along the same path.

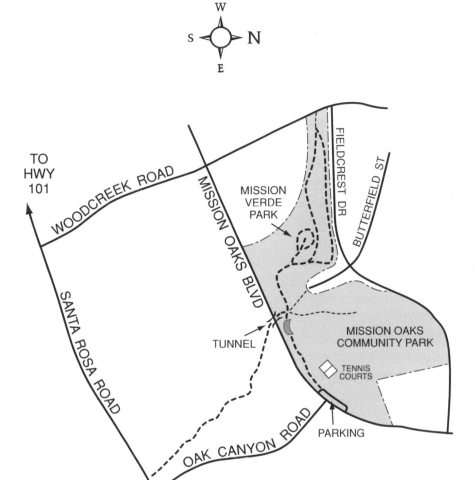

W
N
S
E

TO
HWY
101

WOODCREEK ROAD

MISSION OAKS BLVD

FIELDCREST DR

BUTTERFIELD ST

MISSION
VERDE
PARK

SANTA ROSA ROAD

TUNNEL

MISSION OAKS
COMMUNITY PARK

TENNIS
COURTS

OAK CANYON ROAD

PARKING

MISSION OAKS
COMMUNITY PARK TRAIL

Hike 27
Arroyo Verde Park

Hiking distance: 3 mile loop
Hiking time: 1.5 hours
Elevation gain: 200 feet

Summary of hike: Arroyo Verde Park is a 129-acre park in Ventura. On the south end of the park is a developed 14-acre open grassy area. To the north is a natural, chaparral-covered canyon area. A series of trails lead up the hillsides to excellent vista points above the developed portion of the park.

Driving directions: From Highway 101/Ventura Freeway in Ventura, exit on Victoria Avenue. Head 2.2 miles north to the end of Victoria Avenue at Foothill Road. Turn left and continue 0.7 miles to Arroyo Verde Park, opposite of Day Road. Turn right into the park entrance, and park past the nature center in the first lot.

Hiking directions: The trail begins near the park entrance across the lawn from the Arroyo Verde Center. You may also pick up the trail by crossing the lawn to the west from the parking lot. The trail heads north, traversing the hillside along the forested route. At 0.8 miles, the trail descends at Vista Bluff and meets the park road by Redwood Glen. Cross the road, picking up the backcountry trail, and continue north into the canyon. A short distance ahead is a junction. The left fork, the higher route, loops around the hillside and rejoins the right fork at the north end of the canyon below The Wall. From the end of the canyon, head to the right 50 yards to another junction. The left fork heads up the hillside, returning along the eastern side of the park. The right fork follows the canyon floor, returning along the most direct route. Both routes lead back to the parking lot.

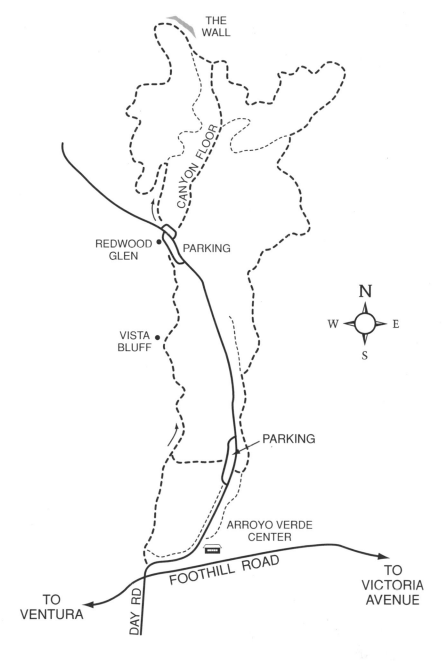

ARROYO VERDE PARK

Hike 28
Santa Paula Canyon

Hiking distance: 6 miles round trip
Hiking time: 3 hours
Elevation gain: 750 feet
Maps: U.S.G.S. Santa Paula Peak

Summary of hike: The Santa Paula Canyon Trail is among the most beautiful and popular hikes in the Ojai area. The trail follows Santa Paula Creek up a shady, forested canyon past a variety of small pools. The hike ends in a scenic, narrow gorge with a 25-foot waterfall and deep pool (cover photo).

Driving directions: From downtown Ojai, drive 11 miles east towards Santa Paula on Highway 150. Park in the trailhead parking area on the right side of the road just east of the bridge, across from Thomas Aquinas College.
From Santa Paula, drive 5.7 miles northwest on Highway 150.

Hiking directions: From the trailhead parking lot, hike 500 feet up and across the road, entering Thomas Aquinas College. Stay on the paved road, heading north towards the top of the campus. Near the top, take the road veering off to the right. Walk through the gate and past Ferndale Ranch. The road ends in front of two scenic oil rigs. The trail curves around to the left, then enters the forested Santa Paula Canyon along the creek. Cross to the north side of the creek, and head up canyon to a fire road at 1.2 miles. Continue up the fire road. The trail recrosses the creek at two miles and begins switchbacking up the mountain. The trail levels off before dropping down into Big Cone Camp. Past the grassy flat, the narrow trail descends to Santa Paula Creek. Head 30 yards downstream to a side canyon on the right. The waterfall and pool are twenty yards up this canyon. Large boulders around the pool are perfect for sitting and viewing the falls. To return, reverse your route.

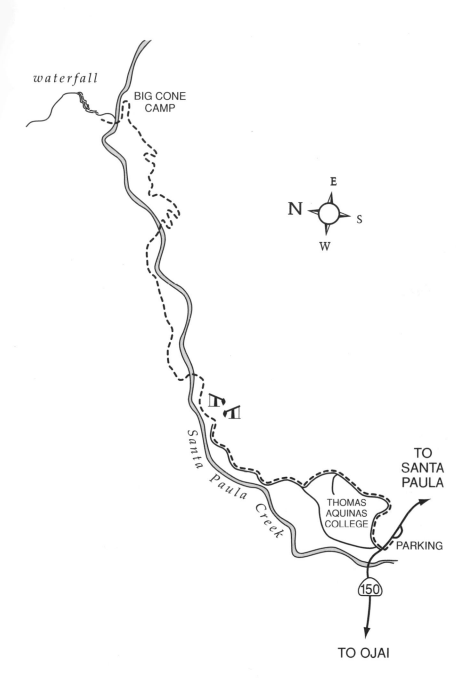

waterfall

BIG CONE
CAMP

E
N ⊕ S
W

Santa Paula Creek

TO
SANTA
PAULA

THOMAS
AQUINAS
COLLEGE

PARKING

150

TO OJAI

SANTA PAULA CANYON

Hike 29
Sisar Canyon

Hiking distance: 4 miles round trip
Hiking time: 2 hours
Elevation gain: 1,000 feet
Maps: U.S.G.S. Ojai & Santa Paula Peak

Summary of hike: Sisar Canyon begins in the Upper Ojai Valley, halfway between Ojai and Santa Paula. The Sisar Canyon Trail follows Sisar Creek through a canopy of oak and sycamore trees up this beautiful canyon. The hike involves several stream crossings and a scenic overlook with views across the Ojai Valley to Sulphur Mountain.

Driving directions: From downtown Ojai, drive 7.8 miles east towards Santa Paula on Highway 150. Turn left on Sisar Road along the eastern side of Summit School. Drive one mile to the trailhead gate, bearing right at the road split. Park on the side of the road.

From Santa Paula, drive 8.7 miles northwest towards Ojai on Highway 150.

Hiking directions: Hike north past the trailhead gate up the fire road. Sisar Creek is to the right of the road. Within minutes, the trail crosses the creek by small waterfalls and pools. The trail steadily gains elevation up Sisar Canyon. At one mile, the trail recrosses the creek. Continue up canyon, parallel to the creek, to a sharp left bend in the trail. The trail leaves Sisar Creek and begins to climb out of the canyon to an overlook and another switchback curving to the right. Although the trail continues, the overlook is a good place to begin the return hike.

To hike further, the trail continues up the ridge for 3.5 miles to White Ledge Camp, eventually crossing the Topatopa Ridge into the Sespe Wilderness.

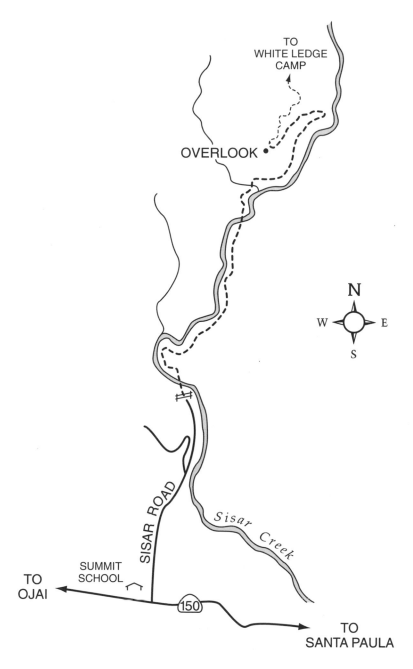

TO
WHITE LEDGE
CAMP

OVERLOOK •

N
W ● E
S

SISAR ROAD

Sisar Creek

SUMMIT
SCHOOL

TO
OJAI

150

TO
SANTA PAULA

SISAR CANYON

Hike 30
Sulphur Mountain Road

Hiking distance: 10 miles one-way (car shuttle)
Hiking time: 4 hours
Elevation loss: 2,200 feet
Maps: U.S.G.S. Ojai and Matilija

Summary of hike: Sulphur Mountain Road, a gated road that may be hiked or biked, follows a 2,600-foot ridge along Sulphur Mountain. The journey across Sulphur Mountain Road has gorgeous alternating views. There are views to the south and west of the Conejo Valley, the Pacific Ocean, and the Channel Islands. At other times are views to the north of the Ojai Valley, the Topatopa Mountains, and the Los Padres National Forest.

Driving directions: Leave a shuttle car at the end of the hike: From Highway 101/Ventura Freeway in Ventura, drive 7.5 miles north on Highway 33 towards Ojai to Sulphur Mountain Road and turn right. Continue 0.4 miles to the locked gate. Park the shuttle car alongside the road.

To the trailhead: Return to Highway 33 and continue north to Ojai. From downtown Ojai, drive 6.4 miles east on Highway 150 towards Santa Paula. Turn right on Sulphur Mountain Road, and continue 4.6 miles up the winding road to a locked gate at the trailhead.

Hiking directions: From the locked gate, hike west along the paved road. At about 1.5 miles, the pavement stops. Continue west along the gradual but steady downhill trail along the mountain ridge. The last two miles are steeper, dropping 1,500 feet. As you near the trail's end, the winding road descends past a cattle guard and gate to the shuttle car parking area at Casitas Springs.

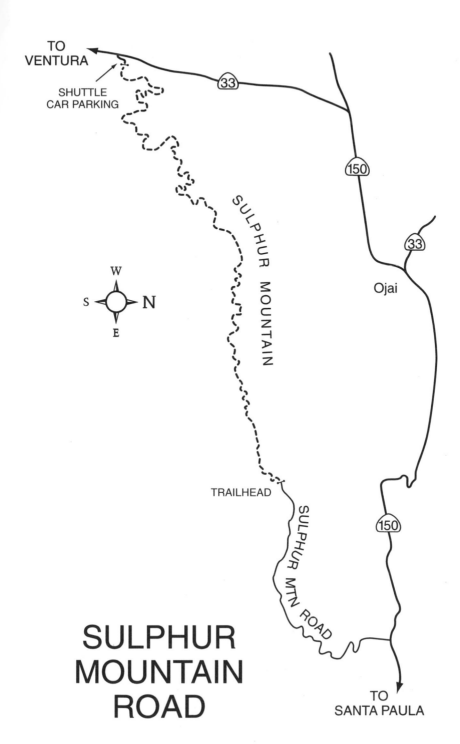

SULPHUR MOUNTAIN ROAD

TO VENTURA

SHUTTLE CAR PARKING

33

150

33

Ojai

SULPHUR MOUNTAIN

TRAILHEAD

SULPHUR MTN ROAD

150

W N S E

TO SANTA PAULA

Hike 31
Horn Canyon Trail

Hiking distance: 3 miles round trip
Hiking time: 1.5 hours
Elevation gain: 600 feet
Maps: U.S.G.S. Ojai

Summary of hike: The Horn Canyon Trail parallels a creek through a forested canyon that is lush with sycamores, alders, and oaks. The trail, which is partially a service road, crosses the creek four times to a rocky gorge. At the gorge, the trail is rugged and far less used, leading past a continuous series of cascades, pools, and small waterfalls.

Driving directions: From downtown Ojai, drive 2.3 miles east on Highway 150 (Ojai Avenue) to Reeves Road and turn left. Continue 1.1 mile to McAndrew Road and turn left again. Drive one mile and enter Thacher School. The trailhead parking area is 0.4 miles ahead, bearing right at all three road splits.

Hiking directions: From the parking area, take the unpaved service road northeast past the gate and kiosk into Horn Canyon. There are two creek crossings in the first half mile. After the second crossing, the service road enters the forest and the trail narrows. At one mile, the trail crosses the creek again and climbs up the west wall of the canyon. There are great views of Horn Canyon and the creek below. At the fourth creek crossing, leave the main trail and take the left path, heading up Horn Canyon along the west side of the creek. The trail is replaced by animal paths that crisscross the creek in a scramble past pools, cascades, and small waterfalls. Choose your own turnaround spot, and return along the same path.

To hike further, at the fourth creek crossing, continue on the Horn Canyon Trail across the creek. The trail steeply climbs out of the canyon to the Pines Campground one mile ahead.

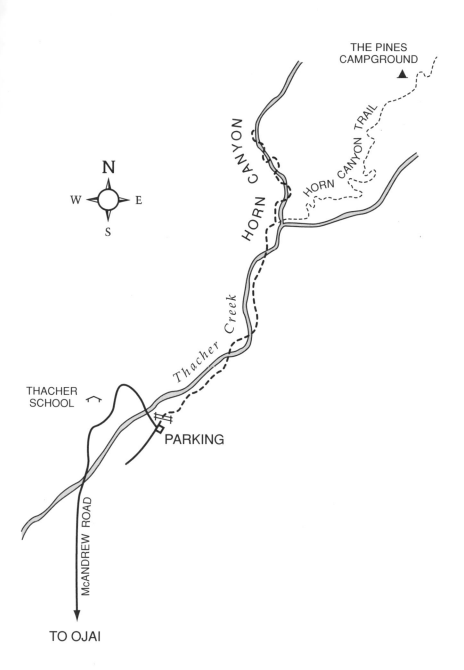

THE PINES
CAMPGROUND

HORN CANYON

HORN CANYON TRAIL

Thacher Creek

N
W E
S

THACHER
SCHOOL

PARKING

McANDREW ROAD

TO OJAI

HORN CANYON TRAIL

Hike 32
Gridley Trail
to Gridley Springs Camp

Hiking distance: 6 miles round trip
Hiking time: 3 hours
Elevation gain: 1,200 feet
Maps: U.S.G.S. Ojai

Summary of hike: The Gridley Trail begins at the edge of Ojai in the foothills of the Topatopa Mountains. The trail follows a fire road into Gridley Canyon along the shady northwest side. Gridley Trail eventually leads six miles up to Nordhoff Peak. This hike goes to Gridley Springs Camp, a primitive campsite by a stream that is halfway to the peak.

Driving directions: From downtown Ojai, drive one mile east on Highway 150 (Ojai Avenue) to Gridley Road and turn left. Continue 1.5 miles to the end of Gridley Road, and park by the signed trailhead on the left.

Hiking directions: Take the signed trail on the west up a draw through the tall, native brush. Continue for a half mile to the Gridley Fire Road. There is a beautiful overlook of the Ojai Valley and Sulphur Mountain on the right. Head to the right up the unpaved, vehicle-free fire road past avocado orchards on the steep slopes. The road curves around the contours of the mountain to a signed five-way junction in Gridley Canyon. Take the center left fork, following the trail sign. At two miles, the trail is perched high above the deep canyon. The trail enters a small side canyon at the confluence of two streams. Gridley Springs Camp is at the first sharp switchback by a horse watering trough. This is the turnaround spot.

To hike further, the trail continues up switchbacks for three steep miles, gaining over 2,000 feet to Nordhoff Peak.

NORDHOFF PEAK
(4,485 feet)

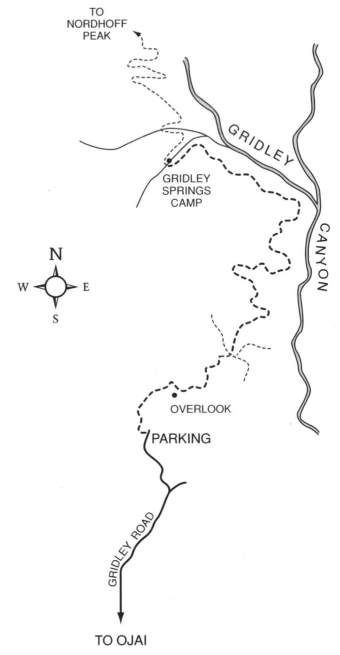

GRIDLEY TRAIL

Hike 33
Shelf Road

Hiking distance: 3.5 miles round trip
Hiking time: 1.5 hours
Elevation gain: 200 feet
Maps: U.S.G.S. Ojai

Summary of hike: Shelf Road is an old, unpaved road that traverses the cliffs several hundred feet above the northern edge of Ojai. The road, gated at both ends, is a hiking, biking, and jogging path that is popular with locals. The path has several scenic overlooks with views of the ten-mile long Ojai Valley, Sulphur Mountain across the valley, and the city of Ojai.

Driving directions: From downtown Ojai, drive one mile north up Signal Street (on the west side of the arcade) to the trailhead gate. Park along the side of the road.

Hiking directions: Hike north past the gate and up the abandoned road. The road curves east, passing orange trees and avocado groves. Shelf Road follows the contours of the cliffs, snaking its way to the east above the city. At 1.7 miles, the trail ends at another entrance gate by Gridley Road. Return to the trailhead along the same route.

For a longer hike, the Shelf Road hike may be combined with the Foothill Trail (Hike 34). The Foothill Trail is a backcountry hike while Shelf Road is more of a stroll.

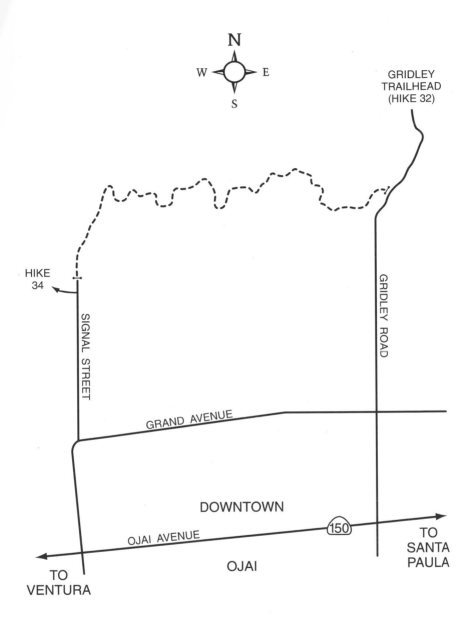

SHELF ROAD

Hike 34
Foothill Trail

Hiking distance: 6 miles round trip
Hiking time: 3 hours
Elevation gain: 900 feet
Maps: U.S.G.S. Matilija and Ojai

Summary of hike: The Foothill Trail runs parallel to the Ojai Valley with stunning views high above Ojai. The trail connects Stewart Canyon on the west to Gridley Canyon on the east.

Driving directions: From downtown Ojai, drive 0.8 miles north up Signal Street (on the west side of the arcade) to the Foothill Trailhead sign by the water tower. Turn left and drive 0.2 miles to the parking area on the left.

Hiking directions: From the parking area, hike west on the signed Pratt Trail. The trail curves to the north up Stewart Canyon and parallels the creek to an unpaved road and junction. Continue straight ahead, following the creek to a second junction. Take the left fork and cross another unpaved road. After crossing, pick up the trail ten feet to the right, heading deeper into the canyon. At one mile, the trail reaches a plateau above the canyon with great views of the Ojai Valley. Stay on the trail as you pass some hillside homes, a creekside rock garden, and a paved road crossing. After a creek crossing, take the unpaved road to the right, following the "trail" signs. Stay on the main road, passing a gate, water tank and a junction with the Foothill Trail going west. One hundred yards beyond the water tank is the Foothill Trail heading east. Take the Foothill Trail east up to a ridge. From the ridge, it is downhill through the canyon to Gridley Road, 100 yards below the Gridley Trailhead (Hike 32).
   To return, walk 0.3 miles down Gridley Road to Shelf Road (Hike 33). Head to the west on Shelf Road for 1.7 miles to the Signal Road gate. The trailhead turnoff is 0.2 miles ahead.

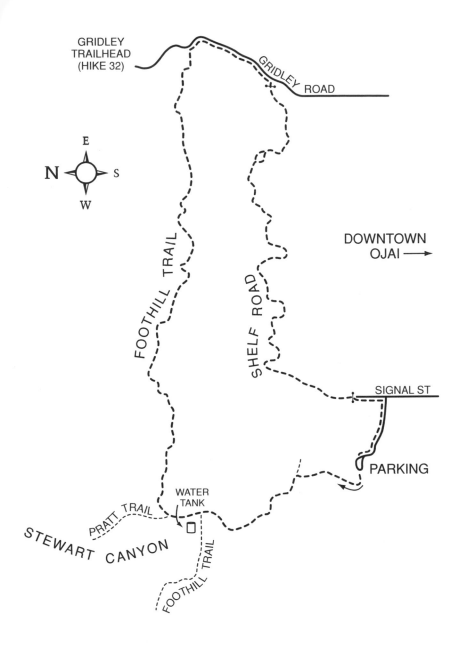

FOOTHILL TRAIL

Hike 35
Cozy Dell Trail

Hiking distance: 4 miles round trip
Hiking time: 2 hours
Elevation gain: 700 feet
Maps: U.S.G.S. Matilija

Summary of hike: The Cozy Dell Trail climbs up a small, shaded canyon to several vista points with panoramic views in every direction. There are great views into the Ojai Valley to the south and the surrounding peaks of the Santa Ynez and Topatopa Mountains. From the overlooks, the trail drops into Cozy Dell Canyon and intersects with the Foothill Trail in a beautiful, forested canyon.

Driving directions: From Ojai, drive 3.4 miles north on Highway 33/Maricopa Highway to the Cozy Dell trailhead parking pullout on the left side of the road. The pullout is located by a bridge, a packing house, and a Forest Service trailhead sign.

Hiking directions: From the parking area, cross the highway to the trailhead, south of the packing house along the right side of the metal railing. Take the well-defined trail east, and head up the canyon. A short distance ahead is a series of 18 switchbacks, gaining 600 feet up the south edge of the canyon. At one mile, the trail reaches its peak at a saddle, giving way to an open area with breathtaking views. Proceed downhill towards Cozy Dell Canyon and back up to a second saddle with more outstanding views. The trail drops back into the trees, descending 200 feet to the forested Cozy Dell Canyon and a junction with the Foothill Trail. One hundred yards to the left is another junction. The Foothill Trail curves to the right and the Pratt Trail heads to the left. This is the turnaround spot. Return by retracing your steps.

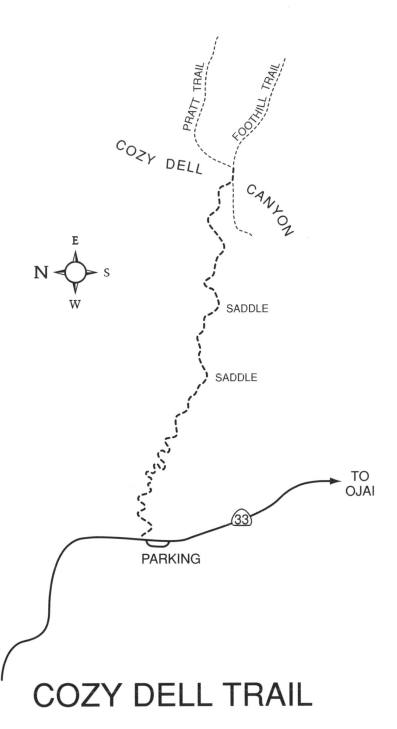

PRATT TRAIL

FOOTHILL TRAIL

COZY DELL

CANYON

E

N S

W

SADDLE

SADDLE

TO
OJAI

33

PARKING

COZY DELL TRAIL

Hike 36
Matilija Camp Trail

Hiking distance: 2 miles round trip
Hiking time: 1 hour
Elevation gain: 200 feet
Maps: U.S.G.S. Old Man Mountain & Wheeler Springs

Summary of hike: The Matilija Camp Trail parallels the Upper North Fork of Matilija Creek in the Los Padres National Forest. The easy trail winds through the lush canyon in the shade of oaks and sycamores. There are three creek crossings en route to the Matilija Campsite, the destination for this hike. At the oak-shaded camp are large boulders, sandstone cliffs, swimming holes, dipping pools, and a picnic area.

Driving directions: From Ojai, drive 4.9 miles north on Highway 33/Maricopa Highway to North Matilija Road and turn left. Continue 4.8 miles to the parking area on the left by the trailhead gate.

Hiking directions: From the parking area, walk up the unpaved road past the gate, a wildlife refuge, and two creek crossings. At 0.5 miles, just past the second creek crossing, leave the road and take the signed Matilija Camp Trail to the right. The well-defined trail heads north, winding its way up the narrow canyon floor between steep, brown cliffs. Cross to the east side of the Upper North Fork Matilija Creek, entering the Matilija Wilderness. Matilija Camp and the pools are between the next two creek crossing. The camp is our turnaround spot.

To hike further, the trail leads to Middle Matilija Camp in another two miles. The trail to the middle camp has several more creek crossings and passes through a wide meadow.

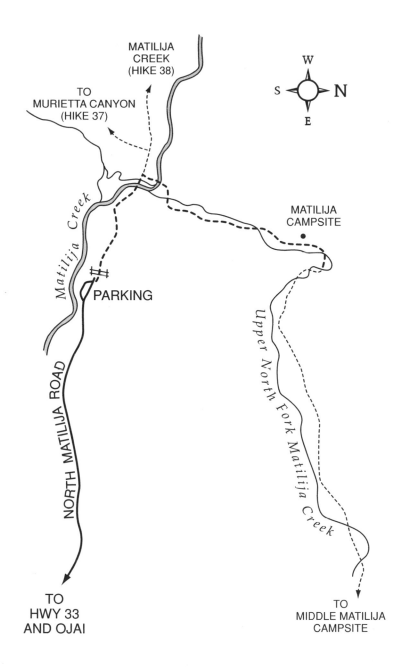

MATILIJA
CREEK
(HIKE 38)

TO
MURIETTA CANYON
(HIKE 37)

W
S ✦ N
E

MATILIJA
CAMPSITE

Matilija Creek

PARKING

Upper North Fork Matilija Creek

NORTH MATILIJA ROAD

TO
HWY 33
AND OJAI

TO
MIDDLE MATILIJA
CAMPSITE

MATILIJA CAMP TRAIL

Hike 37
Murietta Canyon

Hiking distance: 3 miles round trip
Hiking time: 1.5 hours
Elevation gain: 200 feet
Maps: U.S.G.S. Old Man Mountain & White Ledge Peak

Summary of hike: The Murietta Trail enters Murietta Canyon along the creek to a campground on a beautiful, wooded flat. Murietta Camp sits at the edge of Murietta Creek under a forest canopy dominated by cedar and oak trees. There are cascades and pools at the creek.

Driving directions: From Ojai, drive 4.9 miles north on Highway 33/Maricopa Highway to North Matilija Road and turn left. Continue 4.8 miles to the parking area on the left by the trailhead gate.

Hiking directions: From the parking area, follow the road past the gate and trailhead sign. Continue west along the unpaved road, crossing two streams. At 0.7 miles, a short distance past the second stream, is the signed Murietta Trail on the left. Leave the road and head south on the footpath towards the mouth of Murietta Canyon. Proceed to a stream crossing by pools and cascades. Rock hop across the stream channels and up a small hill, heading deeper into the canyon. Murietta Camp is at 1.7 miles. From the camp, several trails lead down to the stream. Return along the same path.

Up the canyon from the campground, the trail enters a dense forest with a tangle of vegetation and underbrush. This unmaintained trail becomes vague and hard to follow.

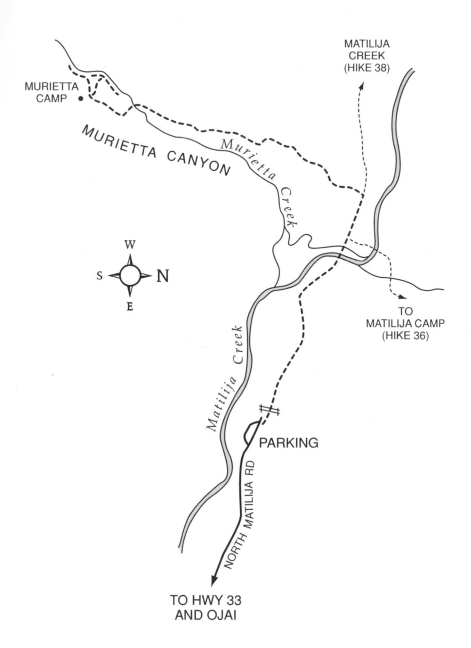

MURIETTA CANYON

Hike 38
Matilija Creek

Hiking distance: 7 miles round trip
Hiking time: 3 hours
Elevation gain: 600 feet
Maps: U.S.G.S. Old Man Mountain

Summary of hike: Matilija Creek leads up the main canyon to beautiful pools, cascades, and water slides. Large shale slabs border the creek for sunbathing beneath the steep canyon cliffs. Up canyon are several towering waterfalls.

Driving directions: From Ojai, drive 4.9 miles north on Highway 33/Maricopa Highway to North Matilija Road and turn left. Continue 4.8 miles to the parking area on the left by the trailhead gate.

Hiking directions: Hike west up the road, past the gate and across two streams. Stay on the main road to an intersection with another trail at one mile. Take the right fork past a house on a Forest Service easement. For a short distance, the trail borders a beautiful rock wall. As you approach the mountain range, cross the stream and curve to the right. The trail follows the western edge of the deep, narrow canyon and crosses another stream. Climb up a short hill to a perch overlooking the canyon. Take the left fork that curves around the gully, and hike down the rocky drainage. Near the canyon floor, the trail picks up again to the left. Hike parallel to the creek along its endless cascades, pools, and rock slabs. This natural playground is the destination. Return along the same path.

To hike further, continue up canyon, creating your own path. There are several waterfalls ahead. Two are located another mile up the main canyon. Another falls is in the canyon to the northeast. This part of the hike is difficult due to slippery shale and an indistinct trail.

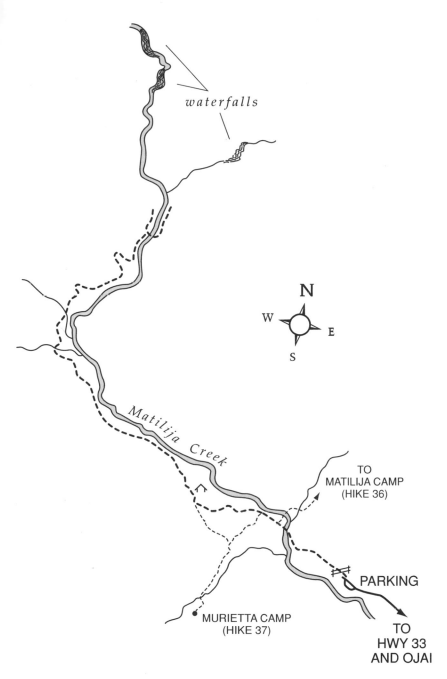

waterfalls

N
W E
S

TO
MATILIJA CAMP
(HIKE 36)

PARKING

MURIETTA CAMP
(HIKE 37)

TO
HWY 33
AND OJAI

Matilija Creek

MATILIJA CREEK

Hike 39
Rose Valley Falls

Hiking distance: 0.8 miles round trip
Hiking time: 30 minutes
Elevation gain: 300 feet
Maps: U.S.G.S. Lion Canyon

Summary of hike: Rose Valley Falls is a 300-foot, two-tiered waterfall. This hike follows Rose Valley Creek up a shady canyon to the base of the lower falls, a hundred-foot, multi-strand waterfall. The waterfall cascades over the sheer sandstone cliffs onto the rocks below in a cool, moss-covered grotto. This short, easy trail begins at the Rose Valley Campground at an elevation of 3,450 feet. There are also three lakes near the campground that are stocked with trout.

Driving directions: From Ojai, drive 14.6 miles north on Highway 33/Maricopa Highway to the Rose Valley turnoff and turn right. Continue 3 miles to the Rose Valley Campground turnoff across from the lower lake and turn right. Drive 0.6 miles to the south end of the campground loop road to the signed trailhead by campsite number 4.

Hiking directions: Hike south past the trailhead sign, immediately entering the thick oak, bay, and sycamore forest on the well-defined trail. Cross the creek and stay on the main path as you make your way up the lush, narrow canyon. The first of several small waterfalls can be spotted on the left at 0.2 miles. Short side paths lead down to the creek by these waterfalls and pools. The trail ends in less than a half mile at the base of lower Rose Valley Falls with its bridal veil beauty. Return along the same path.

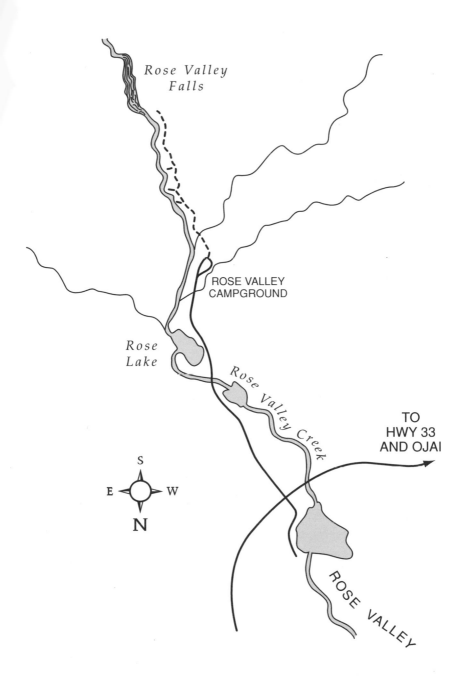

Rose Valley Falls

ROSE VALLEY CAMPGROUND

Rose Lake

Rose Valley Creek

TO HWY 33 AND OJAI

ROSE VALLEY

S
E — W
N

ROSE VALLEY FALLS

Hike 40
West Fork Lion Camp

Hiking distance: 5 miles round trip
Hiking time: 2.5 hours
Elevation gain: 350 feet
Maps: U.S.G.S. Lion Canyon

Summary of hike: West Fork Lion Camp sits along the banks of the creek on a shady flat. Minutes beyond the camp is a beautiful waterfall and deep pool surrounded by rocks. The trail to West Fork Lion Camp heads up the forested Lion Canyon parallel to Lion Canyon Creek.

Driving directions: From Ojai, drive 14.6 miles north on Highway 33/Maricopa Highway to the Rose Valley turnoff and turn right. Continue 4.8 miles to a road split. Take the right fork 0.8 miles down to the Middle Lion Campground and trailhead parking area.

Hiking directions: Walk east along the unpaved campground road, crossing Lion Canyon Creek. Take the signed trail to the right, and head south up Lion Canyon. Continue hiking gradually uphill along the east side of the canyon. At 1.3 miles is a posted junction with the Rose Valley Trail to the right. Proceed straight ahead, staying in Lion Canyon, to another creek crossing at two miles. After crossing is a three-way trail split known as Four Points Trail Junction. To the left is East Fork Lion Camp and a waterfall. Straight ahead is the steep trail up to Nordhoff Ridge. Take the right fork and stay on the east side of the creek along the edge of the rocky hillside. Less than a half mile from the junction is the West Fork Lion Camp. Rock hop up the narrow drainage a short distance past the camp area to a beautiful waterfall and pool. Return by retracing your steps.

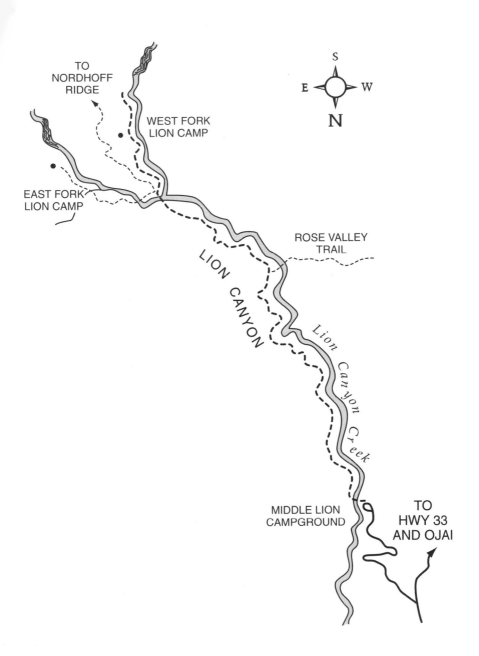

TO
NORDHOFF
RIDGE

S

E ✦ W

N

WEST FORK
LION CAMP

EAST FORK
LION CAMP

ROSE VALLEY
TRAIL

LION CANYON

Lion Canyon Creek

MIDDLE LION
CAMPGROUND

TO
HWY 33
AND OJAI

WEST FORK LION CAMP

Hike 41
Piedra Blanca Formations

Hiking distance: 2.5 miles round trip
Hiking time: 1.5 hours
Elevation gain: 300 feet
Maps: U.S.G.S. Lion Canyon

Summary of hike: The magnificent Piedra Blanca Formations in the Sespe Wilderness are huge, rounded, white sandstone outcroppings sculpted by wind and water. The Gene Marshall-Piedra Blanca National Recreation Trail leads past these massive formations. You can easily spend the day exploring the trails around the unique rocks, cavities, and caves.

Driving directions: From Ojai, drive 14.6 miles north on Highway 33/Maricopa Highway to the Rose Valley turnoff and turn right. Continue 4.8 miles to a road split. Take the left fork one mile down to the Lion Campground and trailhead parking lot at the road's end along the banks of Sespe Creek.

Hiking directions: Rock hop across Sespe Creek. Continue to the trailhead sign and trail junction. The right fork is the Sespe Creek Trail (Hike 42). Take the left fork, heading north towards Piedra Blanca Camp. The trail crosses through chaparral hills past a creekbed to another junction. The left fork heads west towards Howard Creek and Beaver Campground. Proceed to the right, entering the Sespe Wilderness towards the prominent Piedra Blanca formations. At the formations, leave the main trail and explore the area, choosing your own route. Return along the main trail back to the trailhead.

To hike further, the trail continues north, descending into a small canyon and across a stream. The trail parallels Piedra Blanca Creek up canyon to Piedra Blanca Camp at 2.4 miles. Twin Forks Camp is a half mile further.

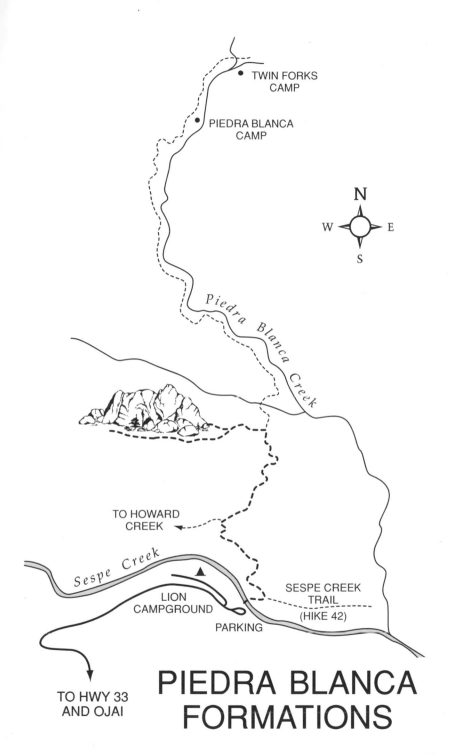

TWIN FORKS
CAMP

PIEDRA BLANCA
CAMP

N
W   E
S

Piedra Blanca Creek

TO HOWARD
CREEK

Sespe Creek

LION
CAMPGROUND

SESPE CREEK
TRAIL
(HIKE 42)

PARKING

TO HWY 33
AND OJAI

PIEDRA BLANCA
FORMATIONS

Hike 42
Sespe Creek Trail

Hiking distance: 3.5 miles round trip
Hiking time: 2 hours
Elevation gain: 200 feet
Maps: U.S.G.S. Lion Canyon

Summary of hike: Sespe Creek is a wide body of water that appears more like a river than a creek. This hike follows a portion of the Old Sespe Road into the Sespe Wilderness to a scenic overlook. The trail parallels the creek past deep pools and sandy flats, crossing Piedra Blanca and Trout Creeks. The 18-mile Old Sespe Road eventually leads to Sespe Hot Springs.

Driving directions: From Ojai, drive 14.6 miles north on Highway 33/Maricopa Highway to the Rose Valley turnoff and turn right. Continue 4.8 miles to a road split. Take the left fork one mile down to the Lion Campground and trailhead parking area at the road's end.

Hiking directions: Cross Sespe Creek and the rocky creekbed, heading north to the posted trail junction. The left fork is the Piedra Blanca Trail (Hike 41). Take the right fork, and head downstream, parallel to the northern banks of Sespe Creek. In a half mile, the trail crosses Piedra Blanca Creek. After crossing, the trail narrows as it enters a canyon. Past the canyon, the trail widens out again and crosses Trout Creek. Along the way, side paths lead down to the creek. A short distance ahead, the trail enters the Sespe Wilderness. The trail gains elevation to a vista overlooking the canyon and passes through a gate. At the top of the ridge, the view opens up to the mountains in the north. The ridge is the turnaround spot.

To hike further, the trail follows Sespe Creek downstream for many miles.

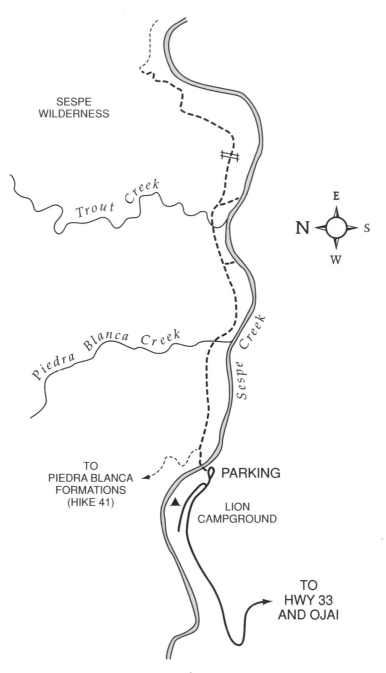

SESPE WILDERNESS

Trout Creek

N ⟡ E S W

Piedra Blanca Creek

Sespe Creek

TO
PIEDRA BLANCA
FORMATIONS
(HIKE 41)

PARKING

LION
CAMPGROUND

TO
HWY 33
AND OJAI

SESPE CREEK

Hike 43
Potrero John Trail

Hiking distance: 4 miles round trip
Hiking time: 2 hours
Elevation gain: 600 feet
Maps: U.S.G.S. Wheeler Springs

Summary of hike: The Potrero John Trail is an uncrowded, lightly used trail in the 220,000-acre Sespe Wilderness, part of Los Padres National Forest. The hike begins at an elevation of 3,655 feet where Potrero John Creek empties into Sespe Creek. The trail follows Potrero John Creek through a narrow gorge and up the canyon. There is also an open meadow dotted with red baked manzanita and views of the surrounding mountains. At the trail's end is Potrero John Camp, a creekside flat shaded with oaks.

Driving directions: From Ojai, drive 21 miles north on Highway 33/Maricopa Highway to the trailhead parking pullout on the right side of the road. It is located on the north side of Potrero Bridge.

Hiking directions: Hike north past the trailhead sign, immediately entering the narrow, steep-walled canyon on the west side of Potrero John Creek. After three successive creek crossings, the trail enters the Sespe Wilderness. There are eight creek crossings in the first mile while passing various pools and cascades. At one mile, the trail leaves the narrow canyon, emerging into a large, open meadow. At the far side of the meadow, the trail ends at Potrero John Camp, a walk-in camp on the banks of the creek. To return, retrace your steps.

To hike further, a rough, unmaintained trail heads upstream over rocks, underbrush, and downfall. Along the way there are continuous pools, cascades, and small waterfalls.

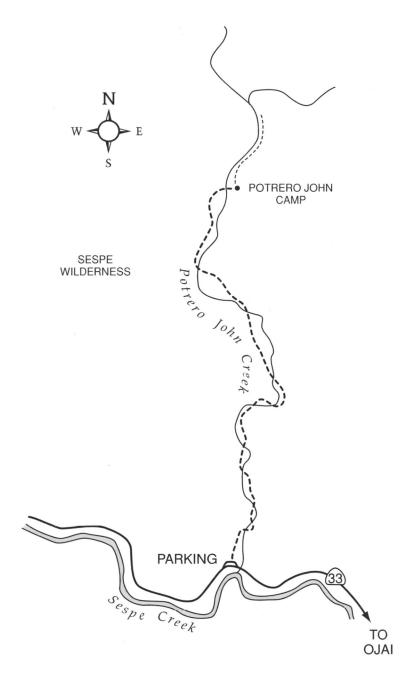

N
W · E
S

SESPE
WILDERNESS

POTRERO JOHN
CAMP

Potrero John Creek

PARKING

Sespe Creek

33

TO
OJAI

POTRERO JOHN TRAIL

Other Day Hike Guidebooks

These books may be purchased at your local bookstore or
outdoor shop. Or, order them direct from the distributor:

The Globe Pequot Press
P.O. Box 833 · Old Saybrook, CT 06475
www.globe-pequot.com

1-800-243-0495